Fantasy Classics

Graphic Classics® Volume Fifteen

2008

Edited by Tom Pomplun

EUREKA PRODUCTIONS

8778 Oak Grove Road, Mount Horeb, Wisconsin 53572

www.graphicclassics.com

AFTER THE FIRE

by *Lord Dunsany* · *illustrated by* *Rachel Masilamani*

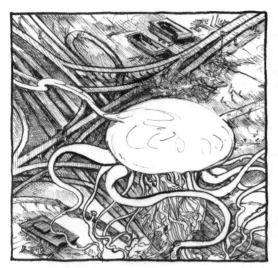

When that happened which had been so long in happening and the world hit a black, uncharted star, certain tremendous creatures out of some other world came peering among the cinders to see if there were anything there that it were worth while to remember.

They spoke of the great things that the world was known to have had; they mentioned the mammoth. And presently they saw man's temples, silent and windowless, staring like empty skulls.

"Some great thing has been here," one said, *"in these huge places."*

"It was the mammoth," said one.

"Something greater than he," said another.

And then they found that the greatest thing in the world had been the dreams of man.

CONTENTS

Fantasy Classics

Graphic Classics® Volume Fifteen

©2008 LANCE TOOKS

Cover illustration by Skot Olsen
Back cover illustration by Leong Wan Kok

Fantasy Classics: Graphic Classics Volume Fifteen / ISBN 978-0-9787919-3-3 is published by Eureka Productions. Price US $11.95, CAN $13.50. Available from Eureka Productions, 8778 Oak Grove Road, Mount Horeb, WI 53572. Tom Pomplun, designer and publisher, tom@graphicclassics.com. Eileen Fitzgerald, editorial assistant. The Dream Quest of Unknown Kadath is adapted by permission of Lovecraft Properties, LLC. Compilation and all original works ©2008 Eureka Productions. Graphic Classics is a registered trademark of Eureka Productions. For ordering information and previews of upcoming volumes visit the Graphic Classics website at http://www.graphicclassics.com. Printed in USA.

Fantasmagoriana: A Prologue to Mary Shelley's **Frankenstein**
by Rod Lott / illustrated by Mark A. Nelson

Geneva. June 1816.
The Summer of Darkness.

It really *was* a dark and stormy night.

Inside the Villa Diodati, five friends weathered the storm.

Lord Byron, poet and host.
Claire Claremont, his lover.
Dr. John Polidori, his physician.
Percy Shelley, poet and friend.
Mary Wollstonecraft Godwin, Percy's teenage fiancée.

LORD BYRON

CLAIRE CLAREMONT

DR. JOHN POLIDORI

PERCY SHELLEY

MARY GODWIN

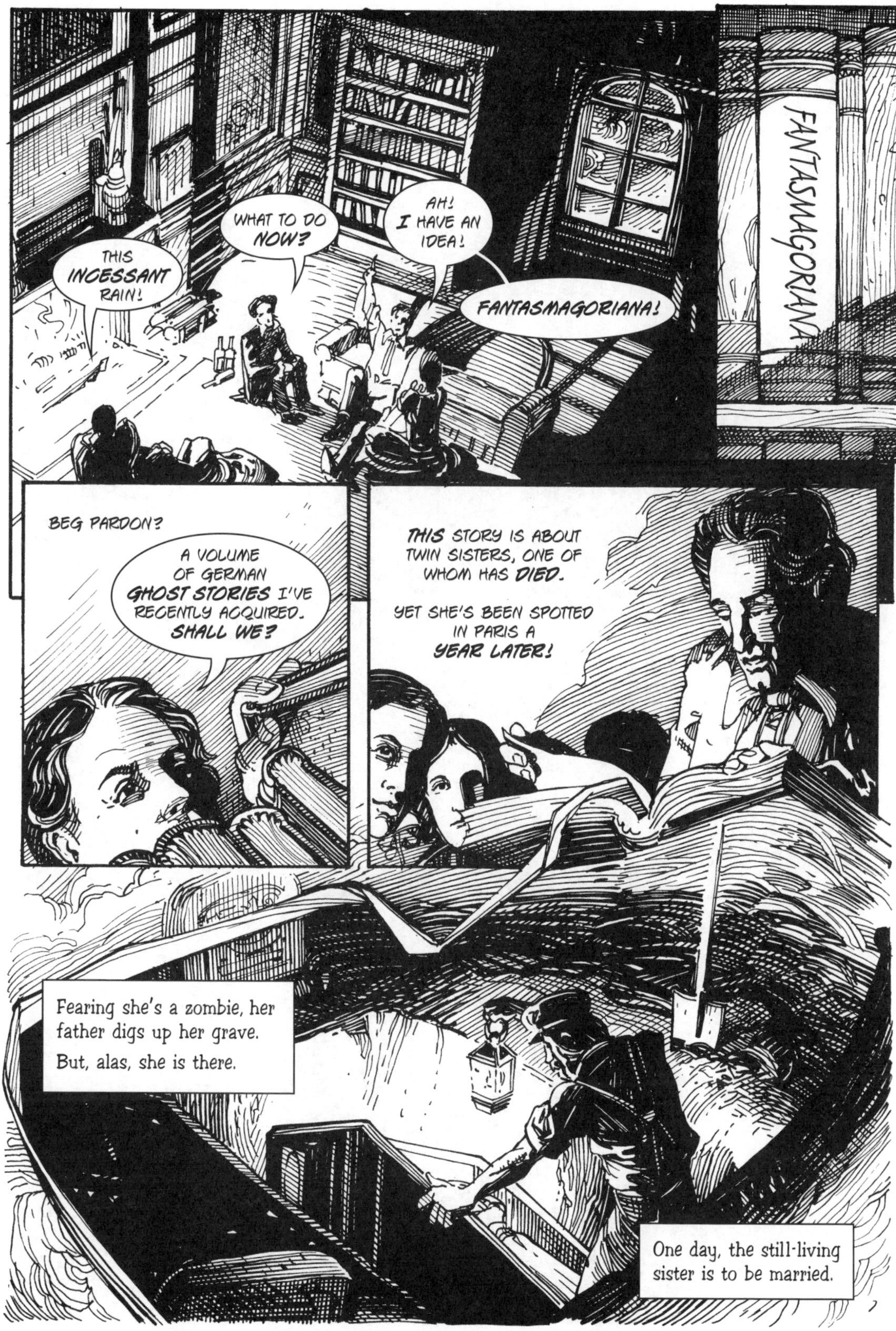
THIS INCESSANT RAIN!
WHAT TO DO NOW?
AH! I HAVE AN IDEA!
FANTASMAGORIANA!
FANTASMAGORIANA
BEG PARDON?
A VOLUME OF GERMAN GHOST STORIES I'VE RECENTLY ACQUIRED. SHALL WE?
THIS STORY IS ABOUT TWIN SISTERS, ONE OF WHOM HAS DIED.
YET SHE'S BEEN SPOTTED IN PARIS A YEAR LATER!
Fearing she's a zombie, her father digs up her grave.
But, alas, she is there.
One day, the still-living sister is to be married.

The wedding goes off without a hitch, until it is time to kiss the bride...

For when the groom removes the veil...

AIIIEEE! I CAN'T TAKE IT!

HOW EXCITING!

LET'S HAVE A CONTEST! EACH OF US SHOULD WRITE OUR OWN GHOST STORY! AND YOU AND I, MARY, SHALL PUBLISH OURS TOGETHER.

BUT I — I DO NOT KNOW IF I COULD EVEN THINK OF ONE!

I CAN!

I HAVE AN IDEA ABOUT A WOMAN PUNISHED FOR PEEPING THROUGH KEYHOLES.... BY HAVING A *SKULL* FOR A HEAD!

AHEM.... *I* SHALL UNDERTAKE A TALE OF *VAMPYRES.*

WHAT ON EARTH?

VAMPYRES — CREATURES WHO ACHIEVE *IMMORTALITY* LIVING OFF THE *LIFEBLOOD* OF OTHERS!

AFTER ALL, WHAT *ELSE* COULD BE THE SOURCE OF LIFE BUT THAT WHICH FLOWS WITHIN US?

WHAT INDEED?

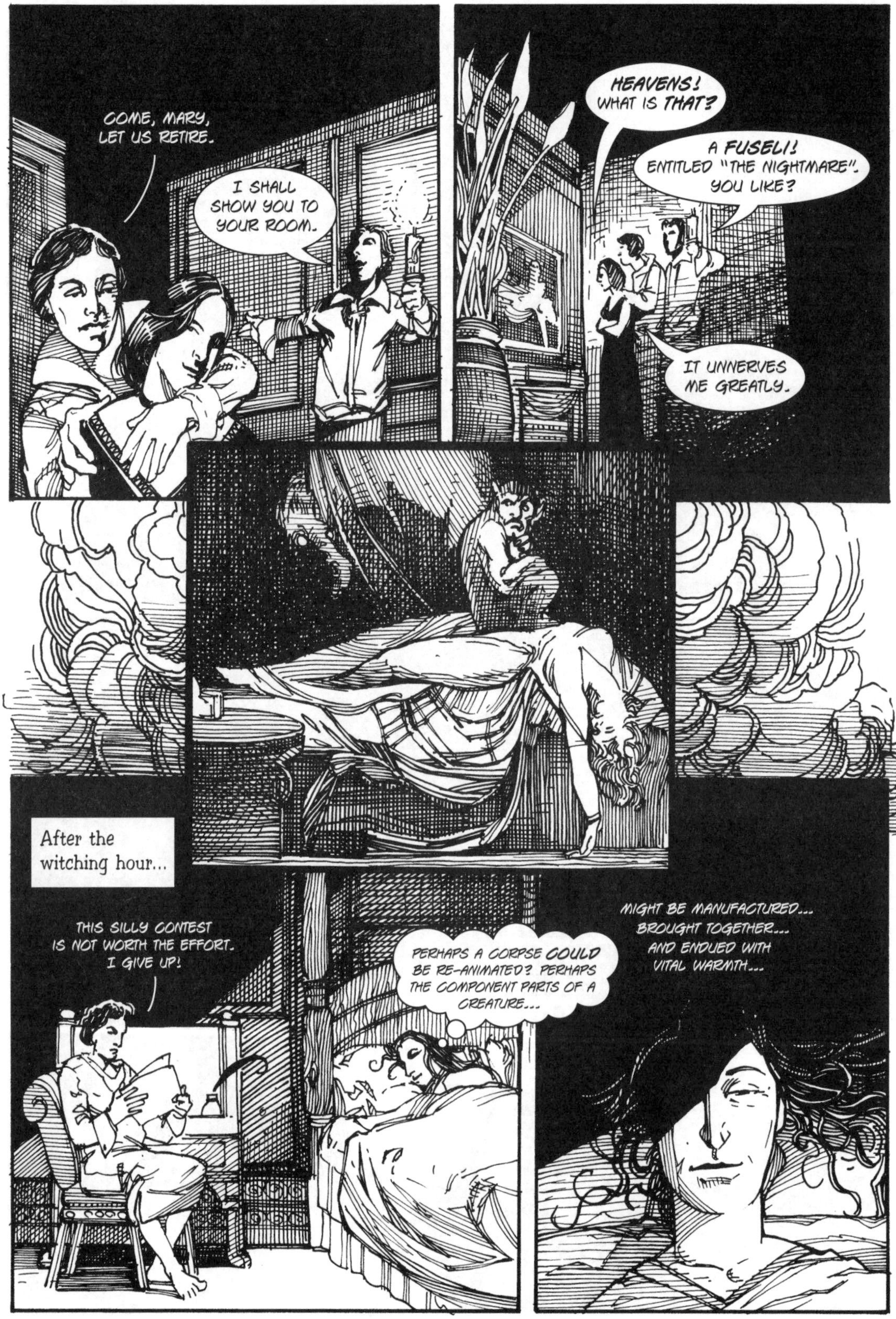
COME, MARY, LET US RETIRE.
I SHALL SHOW YOU TO YOUR ROOM.
HEAVENS! WHAT IS THAT?
A FUSELI! ENTITLED "THE NIGHTMARE". YOU LIKE?
IT UNNERVES ME GREATLY.
After the witching hour...
THIS SILLY CONTEST IS NOT WORTH THE EFFORT. I GIVE UP!
PERHAPS A CORPSE COULD BE RE-ANIMATED? PERHAPS THE COMPONENT PARTS OF A CREATURE...
MIGHT BE MANUFACTURED... BROUGHT TOGETHER... AND ENDUED WITH VITAL WARMTH...

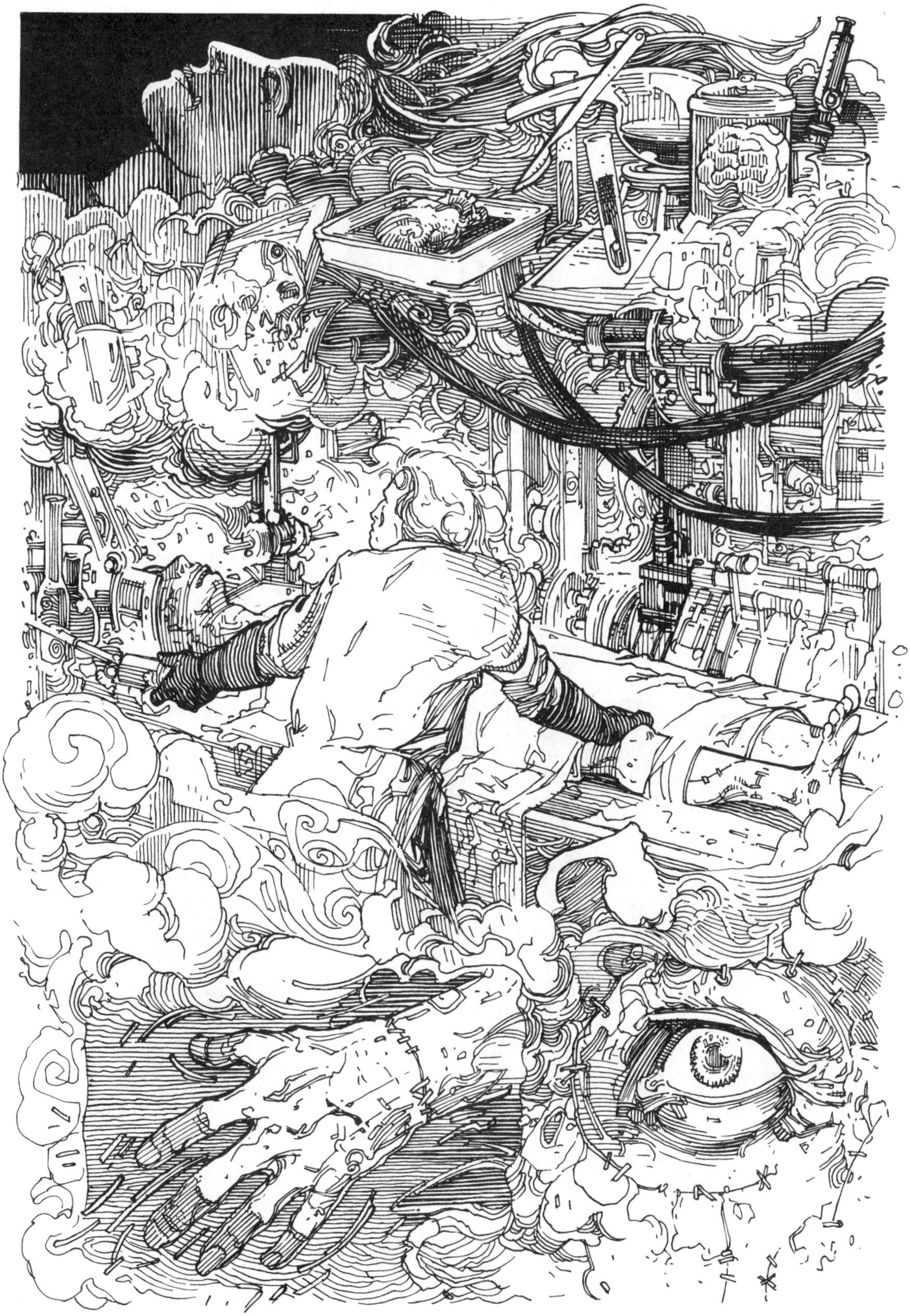

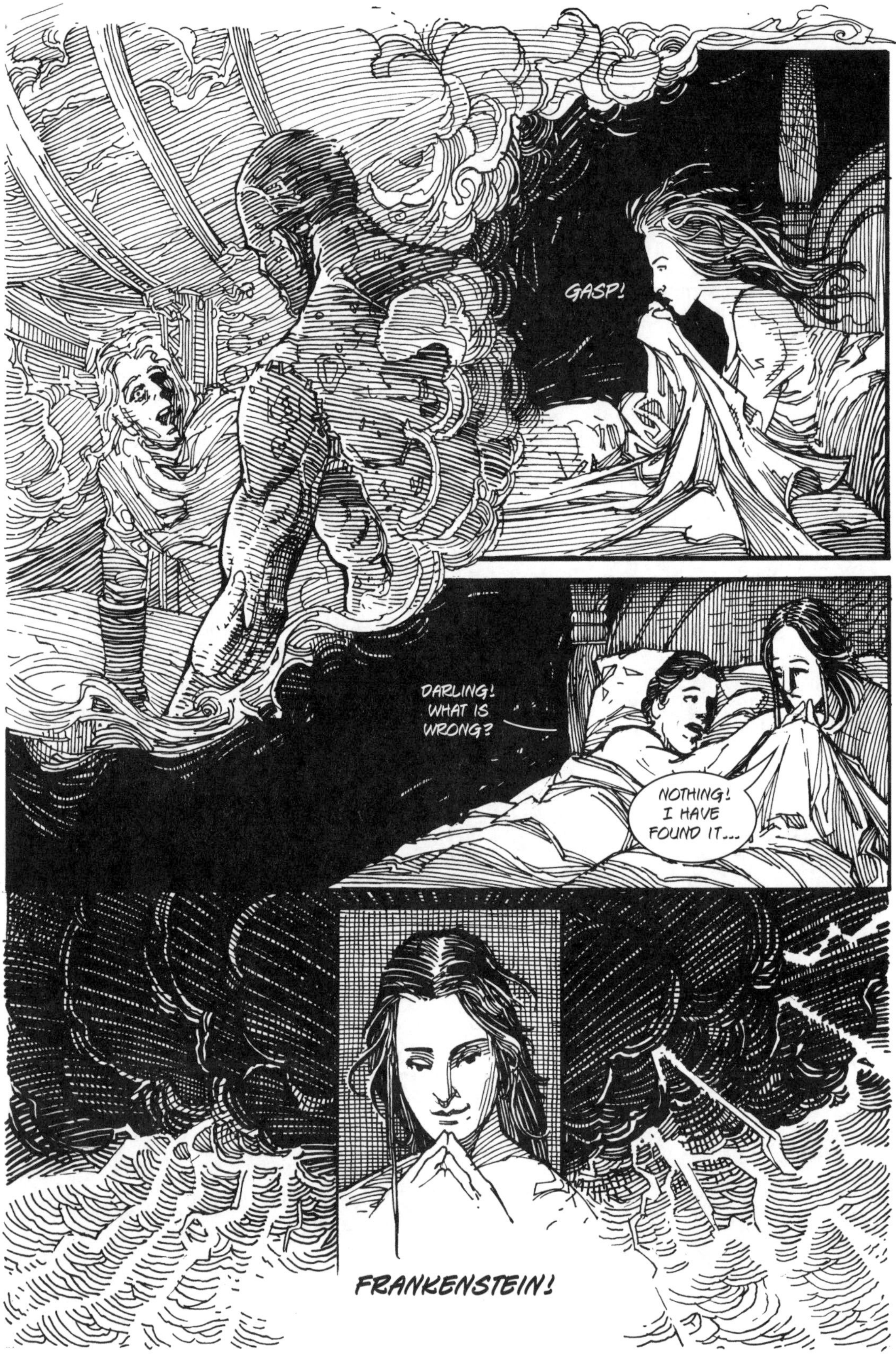
GASP!
DARLING! WHAT IS WRONG?
NOTHING! I HAVE FOUND IT...
FRANKENSTEIN!

MARY SHELLEY'S

FRANKENSTEIN

ADAPTED BY *ROD LOTT* • ILLUSTRATED BY *SKOT OLSEN*

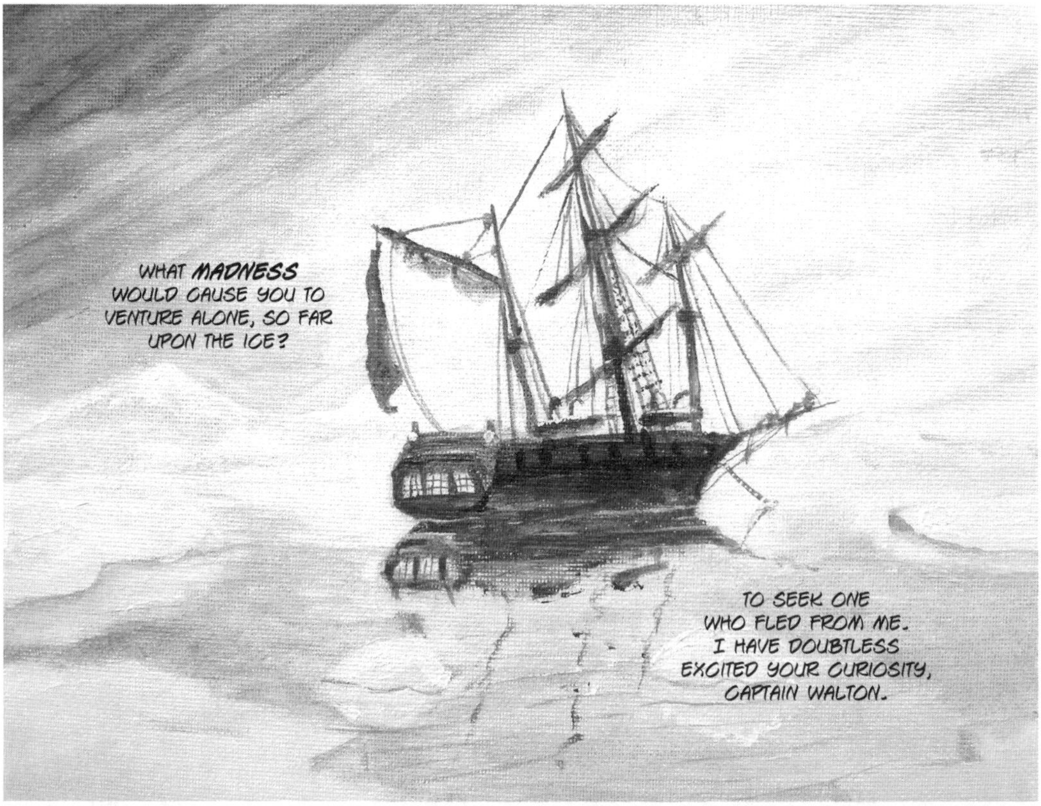
WHAT MADNESS WOULD CAUSE YOU TO VENTURE ALONE, SO FAR UPON THE ICE?
TO SEEK ONE WHO FLED FROM ME. I HAVE DOUBTLESS EXCITED YOUR CURIOSITY, CAPTAIN WALTON.

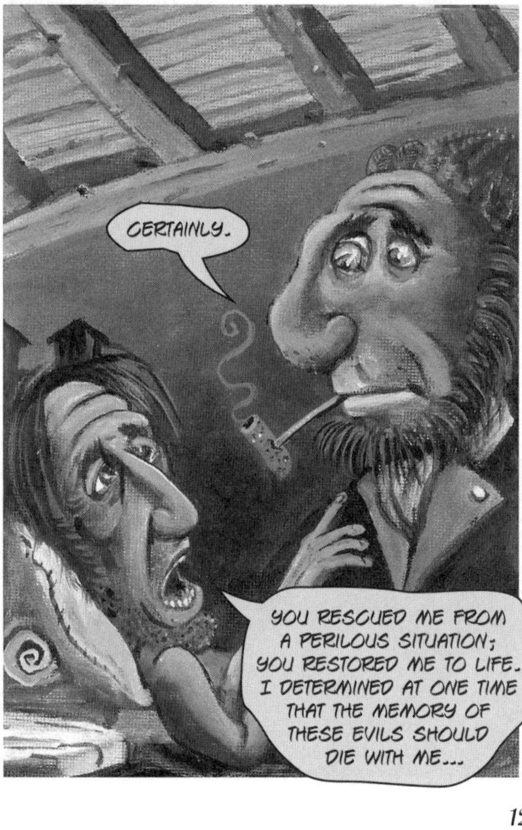
CERTAINLY.
YOU RESCUED ME FROM A PERILOUS SITUATION; YOU RESTORED ME TO LIFE. I DETERMINED AT ONE TIME THAT THE MEMORY OF THESE EVILS SHOULD DIE WITH ME...

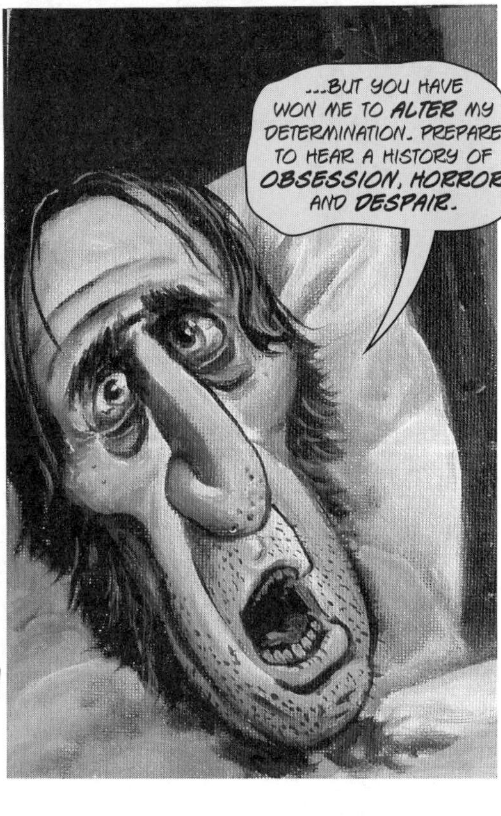
...BUT YOU HAVE WON ME TO ALTER MY DETERMINATION. PREPARE TO HEAR A HISTORY OF OBSESSION, HORROR AND DESPAIR.

"AT UNIVERSITY, I BETOOK MYSELF TO THE BRANCHES OF STUDY OF SCIENCE AND MATHEMATICS."

I AM HAPPY TO HAVE GAINED A DISCIPLE. IF YOU WISH TO BECOME A MAN OF **SCIENCE**, AND NOT A PETTY EXPERIMENTALIST, YOU SHOULD APPLY TO **EVERY** BRANCH OF NATURAL PHILOSOPHY.

"THE PHENOMENA MOST ATTRACTING MY ATTENTION WAS THE STRUCTURE OF THE HUMAN FRAME, AND ANY ANIMAL ENDUED WITH LIFE."

WHENCE DID THE PRINCIPLE OF LIFE PROCEED?

"TO EXAMINE **LIFE**, WE MUST FIRST HAVE RECOURSE TO **DEATH**."

"I SAW MAN DEGRADED AND WASTED — THE CORRUPTION OF **DEATH**. I SAW HOW THE **WORM** INHERITED THE WONDERS OF THE EYE AND BRAIN."

"AFTER DAYS AND NIGHTS OF INTENSE LABOR, I DISCOVERED THE CAUSE OF GENERATION AND *LIFE*; NAY, MORE, I BECAME CAPABLE OF BESTOWING ANIMATION UPON *LIFELESS* MATTER!"

YET TO PREPARE A FRAME FOR IT, WITH MUSCLES AND VEINS... SHOULD I ATTEMPT THE CREATION OF A BEING LIKE MYSELF?

"I RESOLVED TO MAKE THE BEING OF A GIGANTIC STATURE, ABOUT EIGHT FEET. AFTER MONTHS IN COLLECTING MATERIALS, I BEGAN."

"TWO YEARS LATER, I BEHELD THE ACCOMPLISHMENT OF MY TOILS..."

"...AS I INFUSED A SPARK OF *BEING* INTO THE LIFELESS THING THAT LAY AT MY FEET."

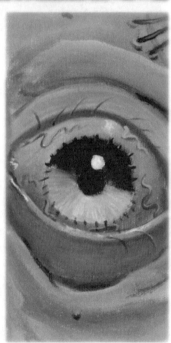

"DEPRIVED OF REST, I RUSHED TO MY BED-CHAMBER. I SLEPT."

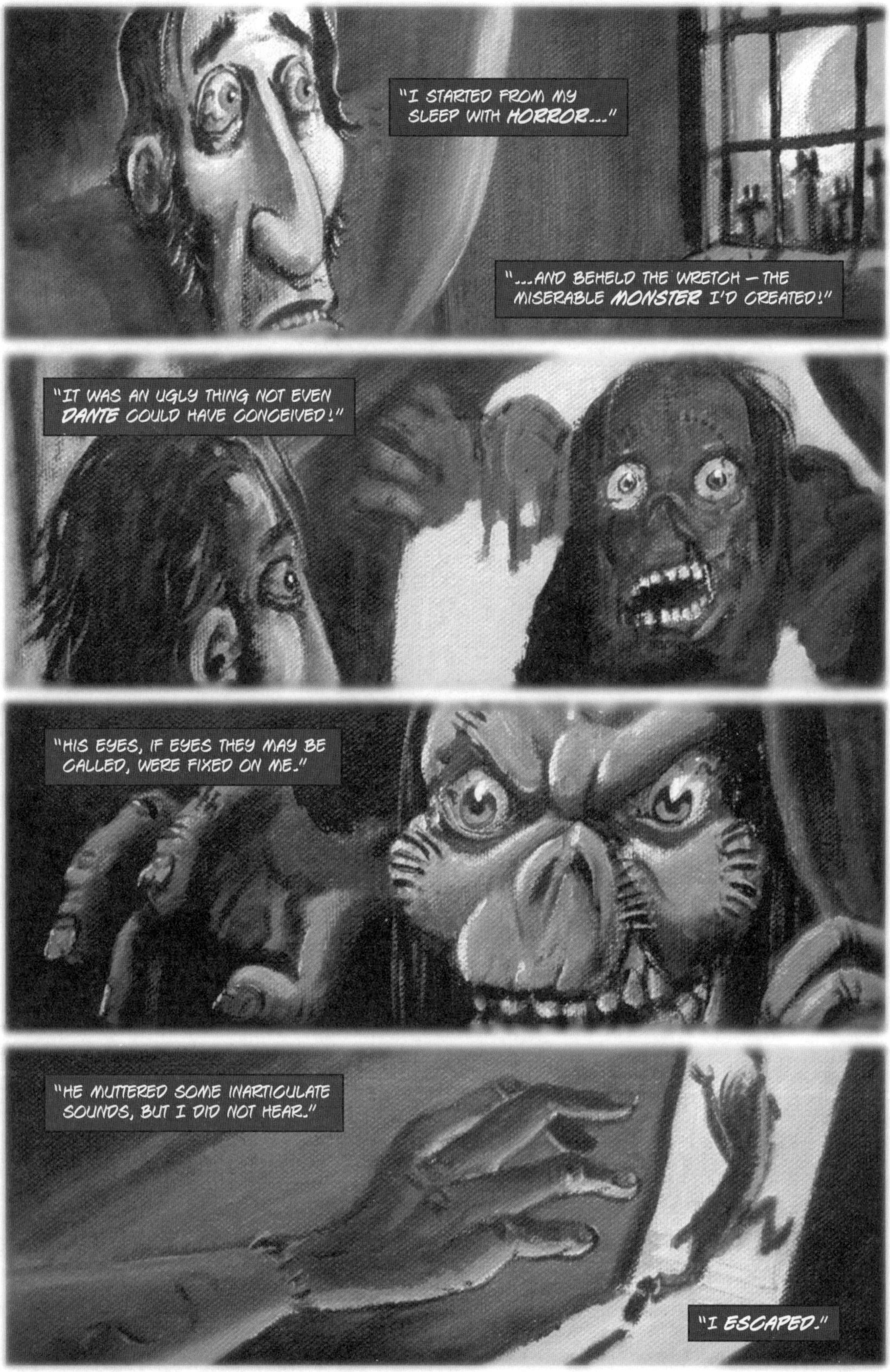
"I STARTED FROM MY SLEEP WITH HORROR..."
"...AND BEHELD THE WRETCH — THE MISERABLE MONSTER I'D CREATED!"
"IT WAS AN UGLY THING NOT EVEN DANTE COULD HAVE CONCEIVED!"
"HIS EYES, IF EYES THEY MAY BE CALLED, WERE FIXED ON ME."
"HE MUTTERED SOME INARTICULATE SOUNDS, BUT I DID NOT HEAR."
"I ESCAPED."

"IN THE MORNING, I WALKED FOR SOME TIME WITH MY FRIEND HENRY CLERVAL, AND FORGOT MY MISFORTUNE."

I HAVE BEEN SO DEEPLY ENGAGED THAT I HAVE NOT RESTED SUFFICIENTLY, BUT I HOPE THESE EMPLOYMENTS ARE NOW AT AN END.

MY DEAR FRANKENSTEIN, HOW VERY ILL YOU APPEAR!

THE CREATURE MIGHT STILL BE HERE. I DREAD TO BEHOLD THIS MONSTER, BUT I FEAR MORE THAT HENRY SHOULD SEE HIM.

HENRY, REMAIN HERE A FEW MINUTES, PLEASE.

EMPTY!

VICTOR? WHAT'S THE MATTER?

DO NOT ASK! SAVE ME!

"THIS BEGAN A NERVOUS FEVER WHICH CONFINED ME FOR MONTHS."

"IN EARLY MAY, I RECEIVED A SHOCKING LETTER REGARDING MY YOUNGEST BROTHER.."

Dear Victor,
William is dead!
He is murdered!

I discovered my lovely boy stretched livid and motionless; the print of the murderer's fingers on his neck.

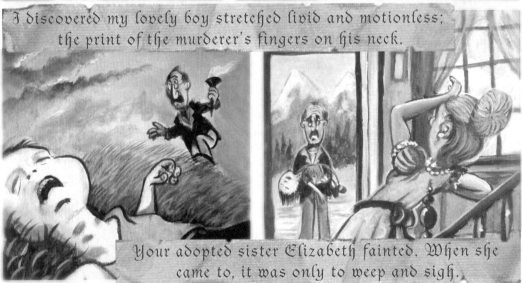

Your adopted sister Elizabeth fainted. When she came to, it was only to weep and sigh.

ELIZABETH!

Come, dearest Victor, you alone can console her.
A. Frankenstein

"I RETURNED HOME AMIDST A RAGING STORM."

WILLIAM, DEAR ANGEL! *THIS* IS THY FUNERAL, *THIS* THY DIRGE!

THE FILTHY *DEMON!* COULD IT BE?... *HE* WAS THE MURDERER!

"ELIZABETH AND MY BROTHER ERNEST HEARD ME ARRIVE."

POOR WILLIAM! BUT THE MURDERER HAS BEEN DISCOVERED.

GOOD GOD! HOW CAN THAT BE? WHO COULD ATTEMPT TO *PURSUE* HIM?

I DON'T KNOW WHAT YOU MEAN. BUT WHO WOULD THINK THAT *JUSTINE MORITZ* COULD BE CAPABLE OF SO APPALLING A CRIME?

JUSTINE IS THE ACCUSED? NO ONE BELIEVES IT, SURELY?

I FEAR SHE WILL BE TRIED TODAY.

BUT SHE IS INNOCENT!

EVERYONE ELSE BELIEVES IN HER GUILT... AND SHE WAS ALWAYS SO FOND OF WILLIAM.

SHE IS UTTERLY GUILTLESS.

"THE LOCKET WITH THE PICTURE OF OUR MOTHER WHICH WILLIAM ALWAYS WORE WAS FOUND IN HER POSSESSION."

GOD KNOWS HOW ENTIRELY INNOCENT I AM, BUT I HAVE NO POWER OF EXPLAINING IT.

"THE JUDGES CONDEMNED THE INNOCENT JUSTINE."

"SHE PERISHED ON THE SCAFFOLD AS A MURDERESS... A VICTIM OF MY THRICE-ACCURSED HANDS!"

MY **ABHORRENCE** OF THIS FIEND CANNOT BE **CONCEIVED!** I WISH TO SEE HIM AGAIN, THAT I MIGHT **AVENGE** THE DEATHS OF WILLIAM AND JUSTINE!

"THE FOLLOWING DAY, I RESOLVED TO ASCEND TO THE SUMMIT OF MONTANVERT. THE SIGHT OF THE MAJESTIC HAD ALWAYS CAUSED ME TO FORGET THE PASSING CARES OF LIFE."

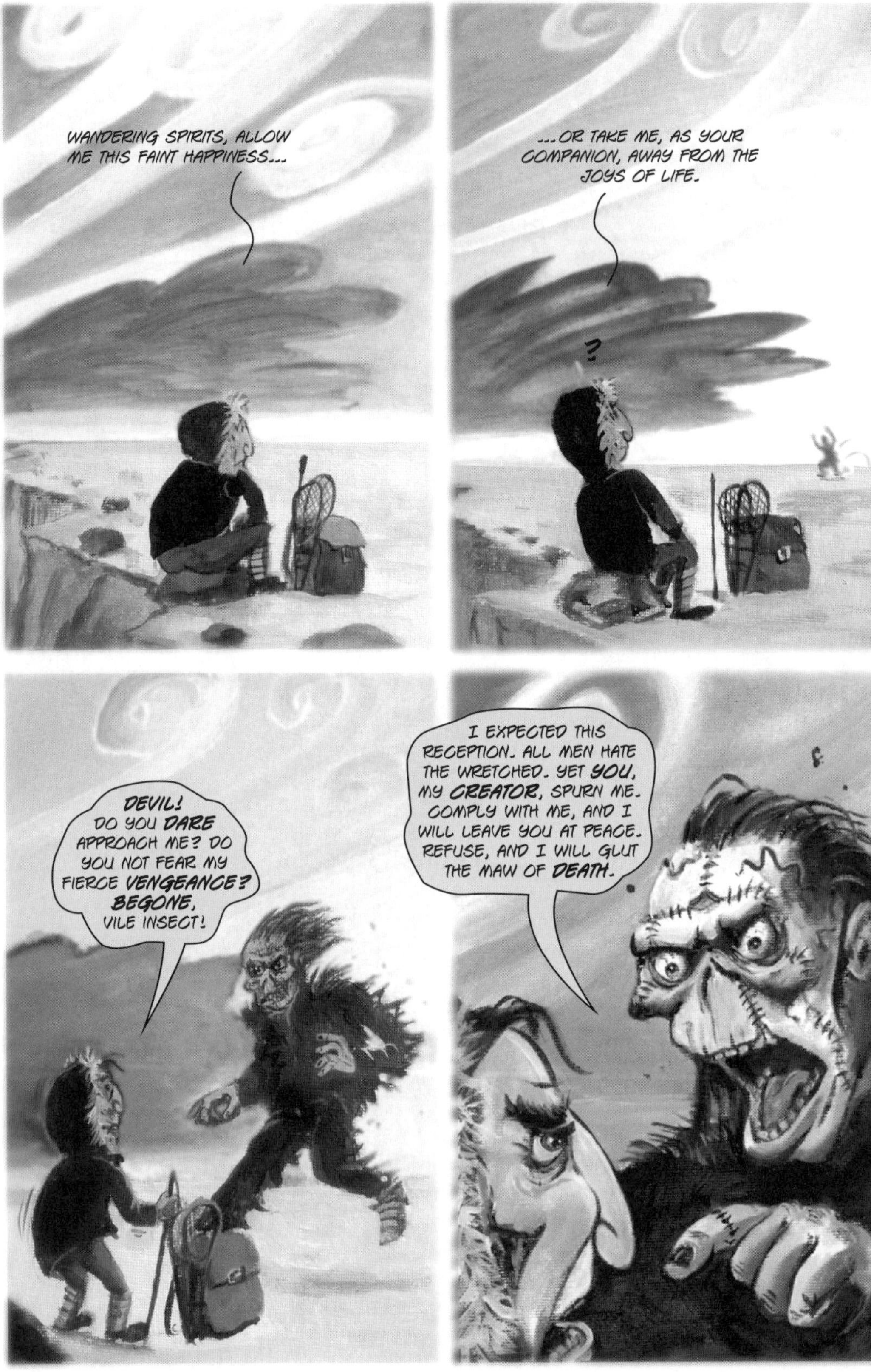
WANDERING SPIRITS, ALLOW ME THIS FAINT HAPPINESS...
...OR TAKE ME, AS YOUR COMPANION, AWAY FROM THE JOYS OF LIFE.
?
DEVIL! DO YOU DARE APPROACH ME? DO YOU NOT FEAR MY FIERCE VENGEANCE? BEGONE, VILE INSECT!
I EXPECTED THIS RECEPTION. ALL MEN HATE THE WRETCHED. YET YOU, MY CREATOR, SPURN ME. COMPLY WITH ME, AND I WILL LEAVE YOU AT PEACE. REFUSE, AND I WILL GLUT THE MAW OF DEATH.

ABHORRED MONSTER! COME, THAT I MAY EXTINGUISH YOUR SPARK!

BE CALM! HEAR ME BEFORE YOU GIVE VENT TO YOUR HATRED!

REMEMBER, THOU MADE ME POWERFUL. I OUGHT TO BE THY ADAM, BUT I AM RATHER THE FALLEN ANGEL. MAKE ME HAPPY, AND I SHALL AGAIN BE VIRTUOUS.

BEGONE!

YOU ACCUSE ME OF MURDER, AND YET YOU WOULD ATTACK ME? OH, PRAISE THE ETERNAL JUSTICE OF MAN! LISTEN TO ME, AND THEN, IF YOU WILL, DESTROY THE WORK OF YOUR HANDS.

COME OUT OF THE COLD AND HEAR MY TALE. IT IS LONG AND STRANGE.

WHEN I LEFT YOU, I STUMBLED IN CONFUSION. EVENTUALLY I ARRIVED AT A VILLAGE. HOW *MIRACULOUS* DID THE COTTAGES AND HOUSES APPEAR!

"I HARDLY PLACED MY FOOT WITHIN THE DOOR OF ONE BEFORE THE CHILDREN SHRIEKED, AND ONE OF THE WOMEN FAINTED!"

"THE WHOLE VILLAGE WAS ROUSED. THEY ATTACKED ME WITH STONES AND WEAPONS."

"I ESCAPED TO THE OPEN COUNTRY AND TOOK REFUGE IN A LOW HOVEL. I FOUND IT AN AGREEABLE ASYLUM FROM THE SNOW AND RAIN."

"WHILE EATING MY MEAGER BREAKFAST, I BEHELD A YOUNG CREATURE PASSING BEFORE MY SHELTER. I STAYED IN HIDING."

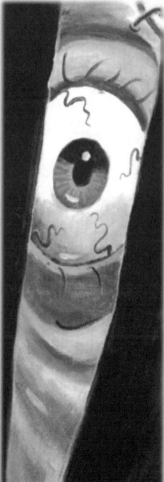

"I COULD NOT SLEEP, THINKING OF THE OCCURRENCES OF THE DAY."

I LONG TO JOIN THEM, BUT DARE NOT.

"THE DAYS PASSED IN ROUTINE. THEY SUFFERED POVERTY IN A VERY DISTRESSING DEGREE."

FROM MY PLACE IN HIDING, I LEARNED THE WORDS "FIRE," "MILK," "BREAD" AND "WOOD." I ALSO LEARNED THEIR NAMES — FATHER, AGATHA, FELIX.

I CANNOT DESCRIBE THE DELIGHT WHEN I WAS ABLE TO PRONOUNCE THEM. I DISTINGUISHED SEVERAL OTHER WORDS, SUCH AS "GOOD," "DEAREST," AND "UNHAPPY."

"I ADMIRED THEIR PERFECT FORMS — THEIR GRACE, BEAUTY —"

"BUT HOW TERRIFIED I WAS WHEN I BEHELD MY *OWN* VISAGE!"

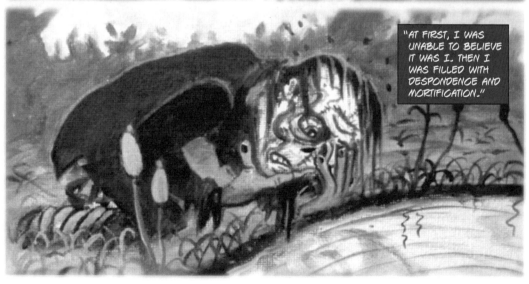

"AT FIRST, I WAS UNABLE TO BELIEVE IT WAS I. THEN I WAS FILLED WITH DESPONDENCE AND MORTIFICATION."

"ONE DAY, A STRANGER ARRIVED, AN ARABIAN. FELIX WELCOMED HER WITH DELIGHT. SHE ENDEAVORED TO LEARN THEIR LANGUAGE."

SAFIE!

"FELIX INSTRUCTED SAFIE. I PAID CLOSE ATTENTION, THAT I MIGHT MASTER THE LANGUAGE."

"THE BOOK WAS VOLNEY'S *RUINS OF EMPIRES*, WHICH INSPIRED ME WITH STRANGE FEELINGS. WHEN I HEARD DETAILS OF VICE AND BLOODSHED, I TURNED AWAY WITH LOATHING."

"THESE WORDS INDUCED ME TO TURN TOWARDS MYSELF."

AM I A *MONSTER*, A BLOT UPON THE EARTH, FROM WHICH ALL MEN FLEE AND WHOM ALL MEN DISOWN?

"ONE NIGHT, I FOUND A PORTMANTEAU CONTAINING SOME BOOKS. I EAGERLY SEIZED THE PRIZE."

"THESE TREASURES GAVE ME EXTREME DELIGHT — AN INFINITY OF NEW IMAGES AND FEELINGS, THAT SOMETIMES RAISED ME TO ECSTASY, FREQUENTLY SUNK ME INTO DEJECTION."

"AS I READ, I APPLIED MUCH TO MY OWN FEELINGS AND CONDITION. I FOUND MYSELF SIMILAR YET STRANGELY UNLIKE TO THE BEINGS WHOM I READ."

MY PERSON IS *HIDEOUS* AND MY STATURE *GIGANTIC*. WHAT DOES THIS MEAN? WHO AM I? *WHAT* AM I? WHENCE DID I COME?

"ANOTHER CIRCUMSTANCE CONFIRMED THESE FEELINGS: I DISCOVERED PAPERS IN THE POCKET OF THE DRESS I HAD TAKEN FROM YOUR LABORATORY...."

...YOUR *JOURNAL* OF THE MONTHS PRECEDING MY CREATION! *EVERY STEP* YOU TOOK IN THE PROGRESS OF YOUR WORK!

THE *MINUTEST* DESCRIPTION OF MY ODIOUS AND LOATHSOME PERSON IS GIVEN. I *SICKENED* AS I READ IT!

WHY CREATE A *MONSTER* SO *HIDEOUS* THAT EVEN *YOU* TURNED AWAY IN DISGUST? GOD MADE MAN BEAUTIFUL, AFTER HIS OWN IMAGE, BUT *MY* FORM IS A *DEGENERATE ECHO* OF YOURS. *SATAN* HAD HIS FELLOW DEVILS TO ADMIRE HIM, BUT I AM *SOLITARY* AND *ABHORRED!*

"LONELY AND AFRAID, I WATCHED MY ADOPTED FAMILY FROM HIDING."

COULD THEY TURN FROM THEIR DOOR ONE, HOWEVER MONSTROUS, WHO SOLICITED THEIR FRIENDSHIP?

WHO'S THERE? COME IN.

PARDON THIS INTRUSION. I'M A TRAVELER IN WANT OF REST.

I WILL TRY TO RELIEVE YOUR WANTS, BUT MY CHILDREN ARE FROM HOME AND I AM BLIND.

I'M AFRAID I SHALL FIND IT DIFFICULT TO PROCURE FOOD FOR YOU.

DO NOT TROUBLE YOURSELF, KIND HOST. IT IS WARMTH AND REST I NEED.

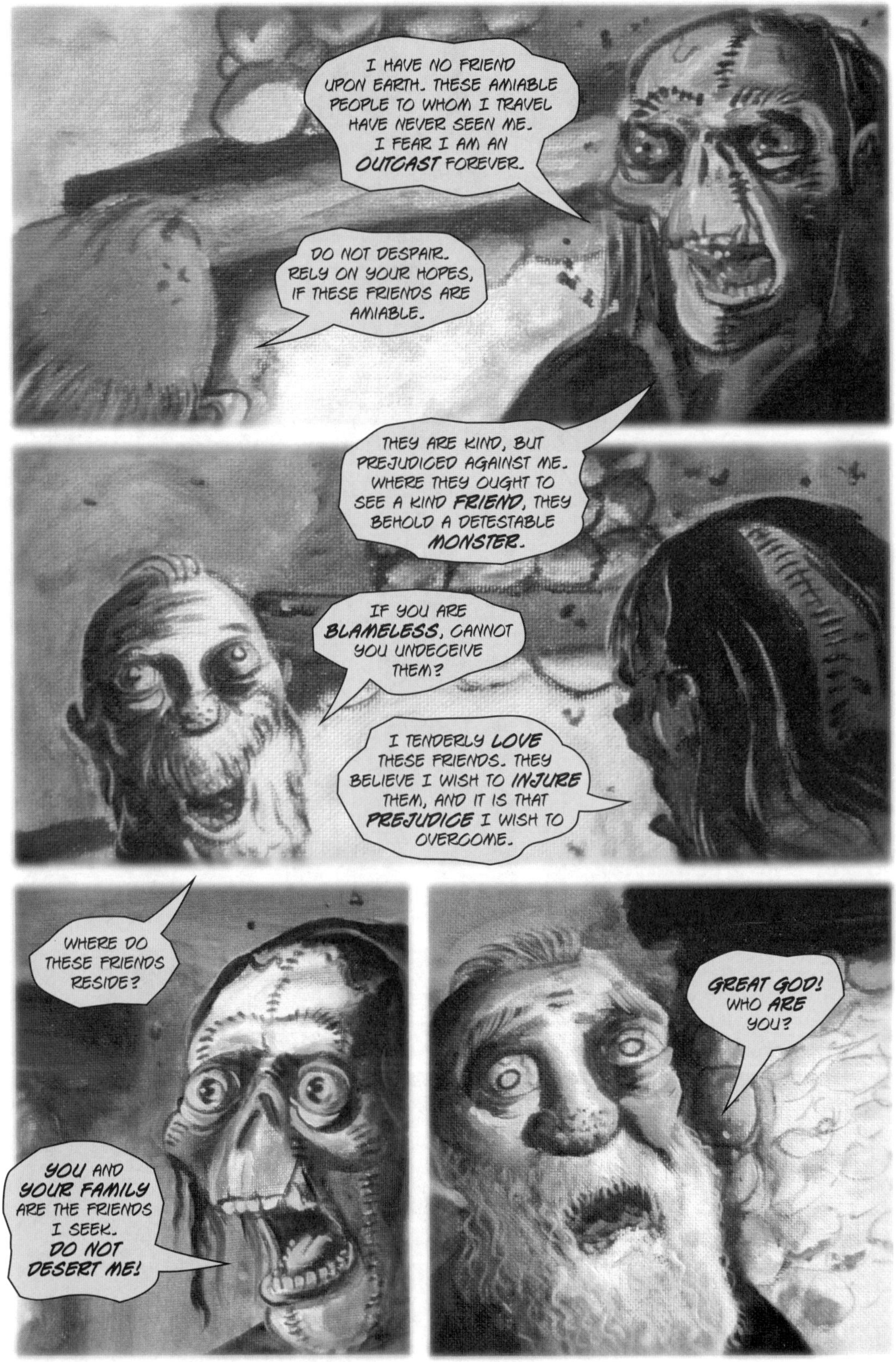
I HAVE NO FRIEND UPON EARTH. THESE AMIABLE PEOPLE TO WHOM I TRAVEL HAVE NEVER SEEN ME. I FEAR I AM AN **OUTCAST** FOREVER.
DO NOT DESPAIR. RELY ON YOUR HOPES, IF THESE FRIENDS ARE AMIABLE.
THEY ARE KIND, BUT PREJUDICED AGAINST ME. WHERE THEY OUGHT TO SEE A KIND **FRIEND**, THEY BEHOLD A DETESTABLE **MONSTER**.
IF YOU ARE **BLAMELESS**, CANNOT YOU UNDECEIVE THEM?
I TENDERLY **LOVE** THESE FRIENDS. THEY BELIEVE I WISH TO **INJURE** THEM, AND IT IS THAT **PREJUDICE** I WISH TO OVERCOME.
WHERE DO THESE FRIENDS RESIDE?
YOU AND **YOUR FAMILY** ARE THE FRIENDS I SEEK. **DO NOT DESERT ME!**
GREAT GOD! WHO **ARE** YOU?

CURSED CREATOR! WHY DO I LIVE?

"MY FEELINGS TURNED TO RAGE AND REVENGE. I BORE A HELL WITHIN ME."

"I HAD LEARNED THE USE OF FIRE, FOR GOOD *AND* EVIL...."

"I TURNED IT AGAINST THOSE WHO HAD REJECTED ME.."

"THE COTTAGE WAS ENVELOPED BY FLAMES, LICKING WITH THEIR FORKED TONGUES."

"THE LESSONS FELIX HAD BESTOWED UPON SAFIE AND MYSELF INCLUDED GEOGRAPHY.."

GENEVA.

"TWO MONTHS LATER, I ARRIVED, AND RETIRED TO A HIDING PLACE AMONG THE FIELDS, OPPRESSED BY FATIGUE AND HUNGER.."

"MY SLEEP WAS DISTURBED BY THE APPROACH OF A BEAUTIFUL CHILD...."

HE HAS LIVED TOO SHORT A TIME TO HAVE A HORROR OF DEFORMITY. IF I TAKE HIM AS MY COMPANION, I SHOULD NOT BE SO DESOLATE.

CHILD, I DO NOT INTEND TO HURT YOU. *LISTEN!*

LET ME GO, MONSTER! LET ME GO OR I WILL TELL MY PAPA!

YOU WILL NEVER SEE YOUR FATHER AGAIN. COME WITH ME.

MY PAPA IS *ALPHONSE FRANKENSTEIN!* HE WILL *PUNISH* YOU!

FRANKENSTEIN! YOU BELONG, THEN, TO MY *ENEMY,* TO WHOM I HAVE SWORN *REVENGE!* YOU SHALL BE MY *FIRST VICTIM!*

"IN A MOMENT HE LAY DEAD AT MY FEET."

I, TOO, CAN CREATE DESOLATION! MY ENEMY IS *NOT* INVULNERABLE! THIS DEATH AND A THOUSAND *OTHER* MISERIES SHALL *DESTROY* HIM!

"TO CREATE FURTHER MISCHIEF, I PLACED THE LOCKET WORN BY THE BOY IN THE HOME OF A WOMAN LIVING NEARBY."

I AM ROBBED BY MY VISAGE OF FEMALE COMPANIONSHIP — THEREFORE *SHE TOO* SHALL SUFFER!

AT LENGTH I WANDERED TOWARDS THESE MOUNTAINS, CONSUMED BY A BURNING PASSION *YOU ALONE* CAN GRATIFY: YOU MUST CREATE A *FEMALE* FOR ME, AS *HIDEOUS* AS *I MYSELF.* I *DEMAND* IT!

I *REFUSE!* TORTURE ME, BUT I WILL *NEVER* CONSENT!

YOU *MUST* DO THIS. IF NOT, I WILL WORK ENDLESSLY AT YOUR *DESTRUCTION!*

DO I NOT OWE HIM THE HAPPINESS IN MY POWER TO BESTOW?

I CONSENT, ON YOUR SOLEMN OATH TO QUIT EUROPE FOREVER.

YOU SHALL NEVER SEE US AGAIN.

"UPON MY RETURN TO GENEVA, I SPOKE WITH MY FATHER...."

AFTER OUR TROUBLES, I LOOK FORWARD TO YOUR MARRIAGE WITH YOUR COUSIN ELIZABETH.

I DO LOVE HER TENDERLY...

EVENTS CAST A GLOOM OVER US. DO YOU NOW OBJECT TO AN IMMEDIATE MARRIAGE?

ALAS! I AM BOUND BY A SOLEMN PROMISE I HAVE NOT YET FULFILLED.

"WITH HENRY CLERVAL AS MY COMPANION, I LEFT FOR ENGLAND, WITH THE AGREEMENT THAT THE MARRIAGE SHOULD TAKE PLACE IMMEDIATELY ON MY RETURN."

"WE TOOK A SHORT TOUR OF SCOTLAND, WHERE HENRY DEPARTED TO VISIT A FRIEND."

"I SOUGHT REFUGE ON A REMOTE ISLAND OF THE ORKNEYS, AND THERE I UNDERTOOK MY DREADED OBLIGATION..."

"AS I PROCEEDED IN MY LABOR, EVERY DAY BECAME MORE HORRIBLE AND IRKSOME. IT WAS A FILTHY PROCESS.."

"A FRENZY HAD BLINDED ME TO THE HORROR OF MY EMPLOYMENT. BUT NOW MY HEART SICKENED AT THE WORK OF MY HANDS."

THREE YEARS AGO, I CREATED A **FIEND** WHOSE UNPARALLELED BARBARITY FILLED MY HEART WITH REMORSE.

MIGHT NOT SHE BECOME EVEN **MORE** MALIGNANT?

THIS CANNOT BE!

YOU HAVE DESTROYED THE WORK! DO YOU DARE BREAK YOUR PROMISE? DO YOU DARE DESTROY MY HOPES? OBEY!

BEGONE! NEVER WILL I CREATE ANOTHER LIKE YOURSELF!

BEWARE! YOUR HOURS WILL PASS IN DREAD AND MISERY. I WILL WATCH WITH THE WILINESS OF A SNAKE, THAT I MAY STING WITH ITS VENOM!

I GO, BUT REMEMBER: I SHALL BE WITH YOU ON YOUR WEDDING NIGHT!

"BEFORE I DEPARTED, THERE WAS A TASK TO PERFORM. I GATHERED MY INSTRUMENTS AND THE ODIOUS REMAINS...."

"...AND THREW THEM INTO THE SEA. THEN I ROWED ON TO THE MAINLAND."

MY FRIENDS, WILL YOU BE SO KIND AS TO TELL ME THE NAME OF THIS TOWN?

YOU'LL KNOW *SOON ENOUGH.* MAYBE A PLACE THAT WILL NOT PROVE MUCH TO YOUR *TASTE.*

WHY ANSWER SO ROUGHLY? SURELY IT IS NOT ENGLISH CUSTOM TO RECEIVE STRANGERS SO INHOSPITABLY.

IT'S THE CUSTOM OF THE *IRISH* TO HATE *VILLAINS!*

YOU MUST FOLLOW ME TO THE MAGISTRATE.

WHY?

YOU WILL GIVE AN ACCOUNT OF THE DEATH OF A GENTLEMAN FOUND *MURDERED* LAST NIGHT!

"THEY SAID THE VICTIM WAS A HANDSOME YOUNG MAN, ABOUT 25 YEARS OF AGE."

STRANGLED, NO SIGN OF VIOLENCE EXCEPT THE BLACK MARK OF FINGERS ON HIS NECK!

LET US TAKE HIM INTO THE ROOM WHERE THE BODY LAY, TO OBSERVE WHAT EFFECT THE SIGHT OF IT WILL PRODUCE.

HENRY CLERVAL, MY *FRIEND!* HAVE MY MURDEROUS MACHINATIONS DEPRIVED *YOU ALSO* OF LIFE?

"HENRY HAD COME SEEKING ME, BUT MET WITH MY CREATION. I KNEW THAT A DANK PRISON CELL WAS MORE THAN MY DUE."

YOU HAVE A VISITOR.

FATHER! ARE YOU SAFE? AND ELIZABETH AND ERNEST?

"HE CALMED ME WITH ASSURANCES OF THEIR WELFARE."

"THE GRAND JURY REJECTED MY CASE, AND I WAS LIBERATED FROM PRISON..."

HOW LITTLE YOU KNOW ME, FATHER. WILLIAM, JUSTINE, HENRY — THEY ALL DIED BY MY HANDS!

I AM NOT MAD! THEY DIED BY MY MACHINATIONS!

MY DEAR SON, NEVER MAKE SUCH AN ASSERTION!

HIS IDEAS ARE DERANGED.

"WE RETURNED TO GENEVA. SWEET ELIZABETH WELCOMED ME WITH WARM AFFECTION..."

"YET SHE WAS THINNER AND HAD LOST MUCH OF HER HEAVENLY VIVACITY."

I WILL CONSECRATE MYSELF, IN LIFE OR DEATH, TO HER HAPPINESS.

DEAR VICTOR, DO NOT SPEAK THUS. HEAVY MISFORTUNES HAVE ALREADY BEFALLEN!

"ALL SMILED ON OUR NUPTIALS, AND ON OUR LAST MOMENTS OF HAPPINESS..."

"AFTER THE CEREMONY, WE TRAVELED TO ELIZABETH'S PROPERTY AT VILLA LAVENZA, WHERE WE PLANNED TO SPEND SOME TIME IN RELAXATION..."

MY LOVE, LET ME TASTE THE QUIET AND FREEDOM FROM DESPAIR THIS ONE DAY PERMITS ME.

"AS SOON AS NIGHT OBSCURED THE SHAPES OF OBJECTS, A THOUSAND FEARS AROSE IN MY MIND..."

"EVERY SOUND TERRIFIED ME."

WHAT IS IT, VICTOR?

PEACE, MY LOVE. ALL WILL BE SAFE, BUT THIS NIGHT IS *DREADFUL!*

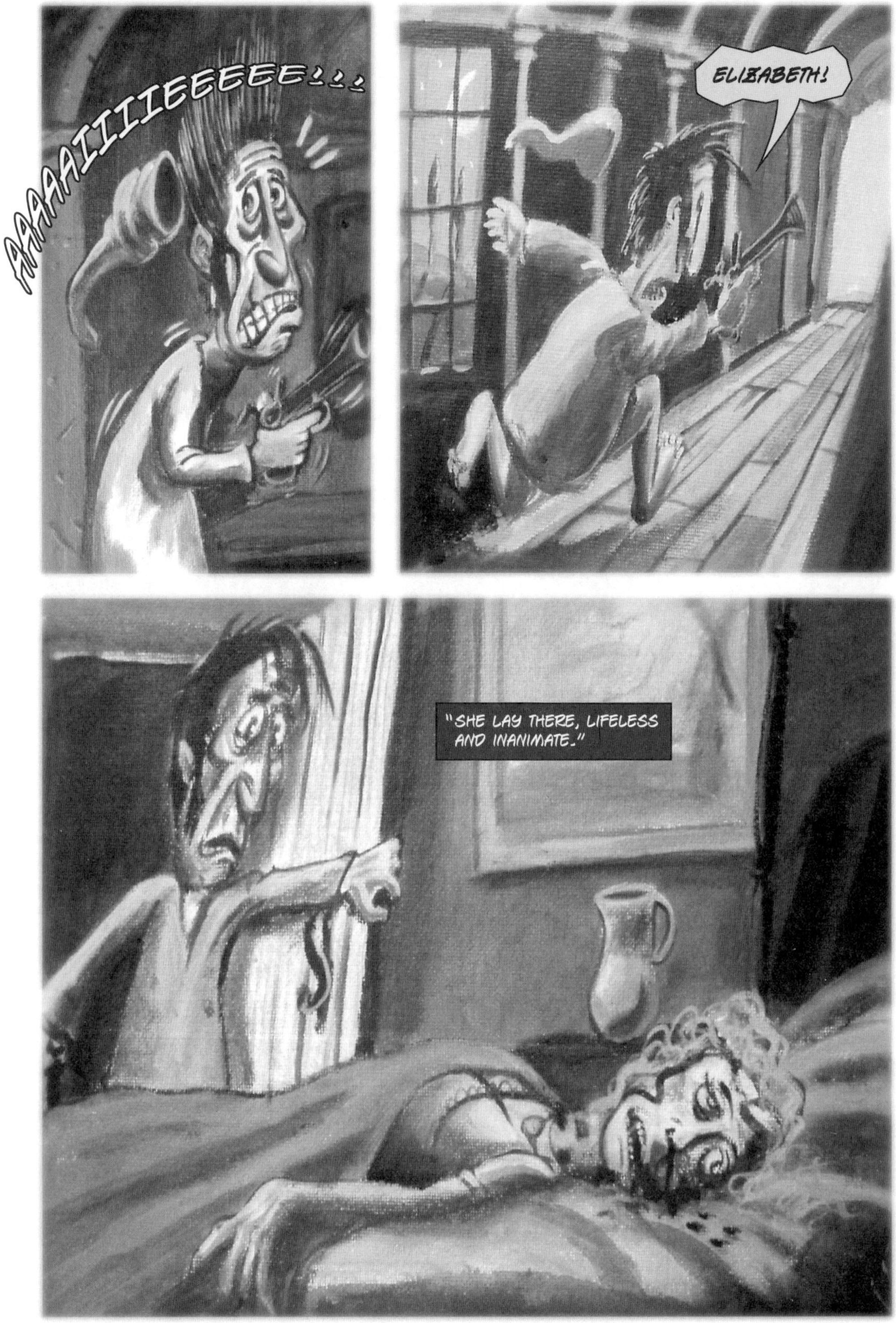
AAAAAIIIIEEEEEE!!!
ELIZABETH!
"SHE LAY THERE, LIFELESS AND INANIMATE."

"THE COLDNESS OF HER LIMBS TOLD ME WHAT I HELD IN MY ARMS CEASED TO BE THE ELIZABETH I CHERISHED.."

"THE MURDEROUS MARK OF THE FIEND'S GRASP WAS ON HER NECK.."

"WITH HORROR, I TURNED AND SAW AT THE WINDOW THE MOST HIDEOUS FIGURE.."

"HE SEEMED TO JEER, AS WITH HIS FIENDISH FINGER HE POINTED TOWARD HER CORPSE..."

BLAM!

"I FIRED, BUT HE ELUDED ME, RUNNING WITH THE SWIFTNESS OF LIGHTNING."

WILLIAM, JUSTINE, CLERVAL, MY WIFE... MY FEW REMAINING FRIENDS ARE NOT SAFE FROM THE MALIGNITY OF THE FIEND.

FATHER! I MUST RETURN TO GENEVA WITH SPEED!

"MY FATHER YET LIVED, BUT SUNK UNDER THE TIDINGS I BORE. IN A FEW DAYS, HE DIED IN MY ARMS."

"I TOLD A CRIMINAL JUDGE THAT I KNEW THE DESTROYER OF MY FAMILY AND I RELATED MY HISTORY."

THIS BEING I ACCUSE. I CALL UPON YOU TO EXERT YOUR WHOLE POWER TO APPREHEND HIM.

I WILL EXERT MYSELF, BUT I FEAR THIS WILL PROVE IMPRACTICABLE!

THEN YOU DO NOT INTEND TO *PURSUE* MY ENEMY!

PERHAPS IT WOULD BE BEST IF YOU SAW A PHYSICIAN....

YOU *REFUSE* MY DEMAND; I HAVE BUT ONE RECOURSE: I *DEVOTE* MYSELF, IN LIFE OR DEATH, TO HIS *DESTRUCTION!*

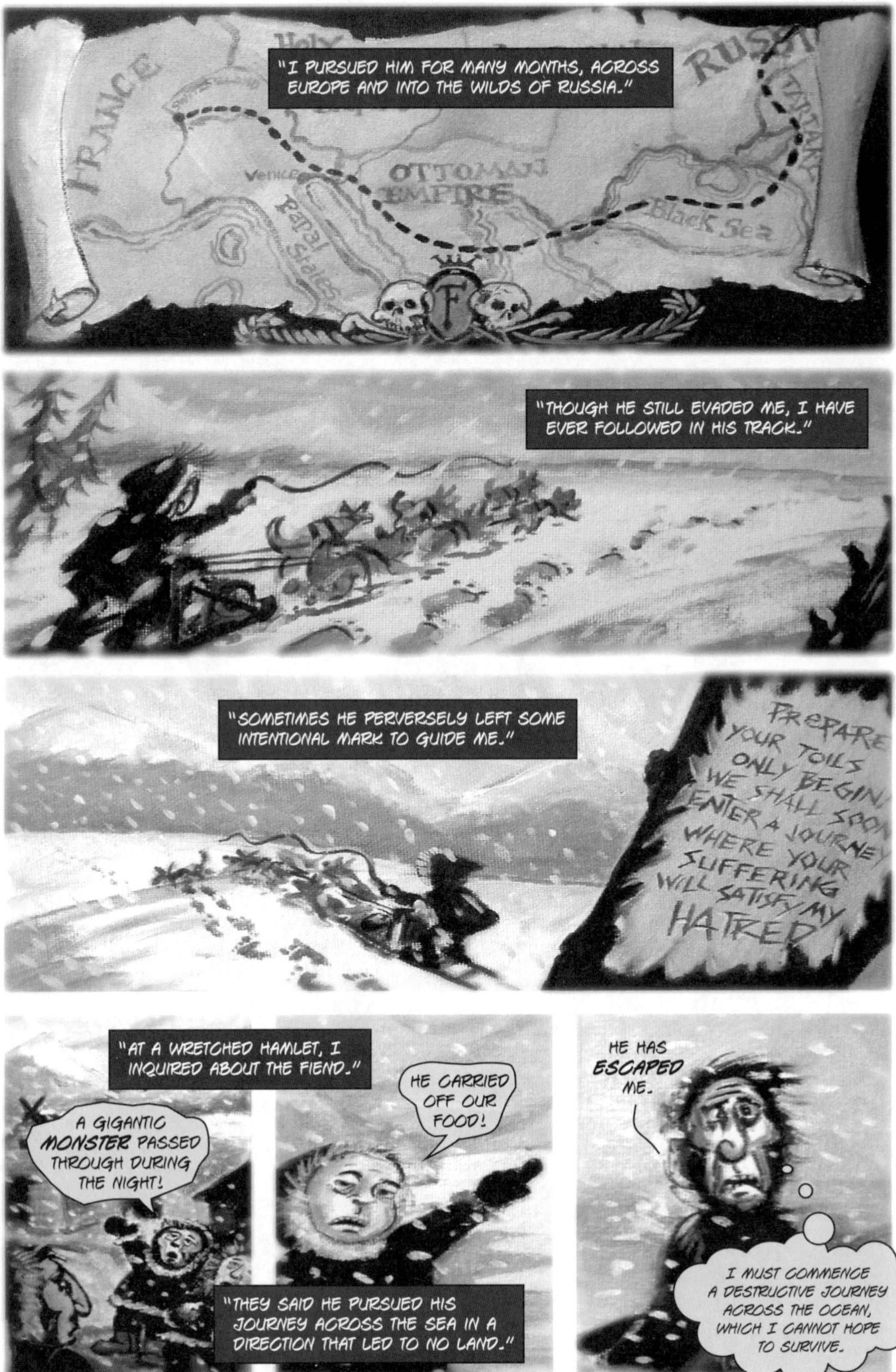
"I PURSUED HIM FOR MANY MONTHS, ACROSS EUROPE AND INTO THE WILDS OF RUSSIA."
FRANCE
Venice
Papal States
OTTOMAN EMPIRE
Black Sea
TARTARY
F
"THOUGH HE STILL EVADED ME, I HAVE EVER FOLLOWED IN HIS TRACK."
"SOMETIMES HE PERVERSELY LEFT SOME INTENTIONAL MARK TO GUIDE ME."
PREPARE YOUR TOILS ONLY BEGIN WE SHALL SOON ENTER A JOURNEY WHERE YOUR SUFFERING WILL SATISFY MY HATRED
"AT A WRETCHED HAMLET, I INQUIRED ABOUT THE FIEND."
A GIGANTIC MONSTER PASSED THROUGH DURING THE NIGHT!
HE CARRIED OFF OUR FOOD!
"THEY SAID HE PURSUED HIS JOURNEY ACROSS THE SEA IN A DIRECTION THAT LED TO NO LAND."
HE HAS ESCAPED ME.
I MUST COMMENCE A DESTRUCTIVE JOURNEY ACROSS THE OCEAN, WHICH I CANNOT HOPE TO SURVIVE.

"I SET OUT IN WHAT I KNEW WOULD BE THE FINAL LEG OF MY PURSUIT."

"I WAS NEAR FROZEN, AND IN DESPAIR WHEN, ON THE FAR HORIZON, I SPOTTED HIS HULKING FIGURE."

"I MADE A MAD DASH FOR IT, BUT AT THAT MOMENT THE ICE CRACKED..."

"...AND I WAS LEFT DRIFTING ON A FLOE CONTINUALLY LESSENING AND PREPARING ME FOR A HIDEOUS DEATH."

"MANY APPALLING HOURS PASSED; SEVERAL DOGS DIED. I MYSELF WAS ABOUT TO SINK WHEN...."

...I SAW YOUR VESSEL.

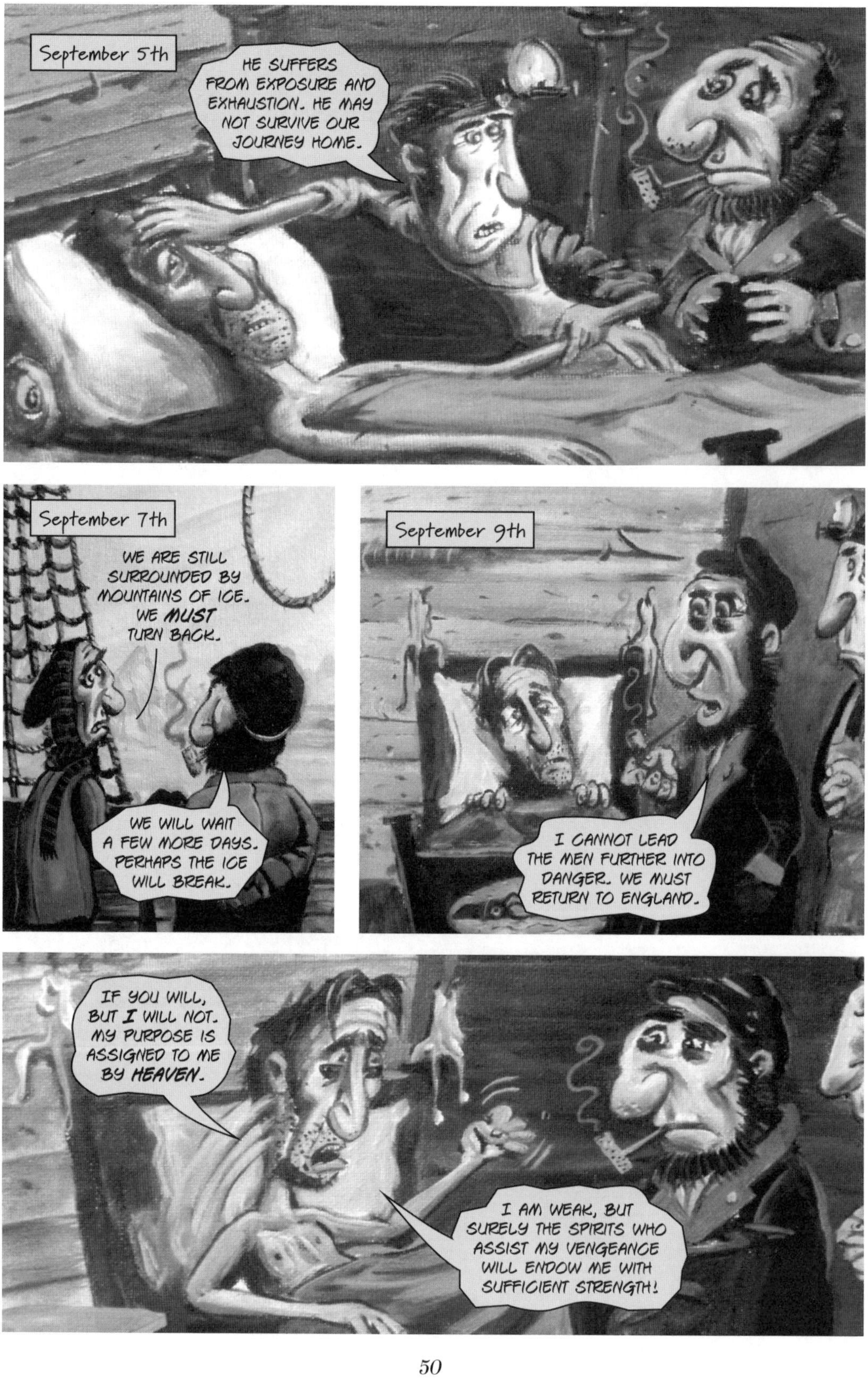
September 5th
HE SUFFERS FROM EXPOSURE AND EXHAUSTION. HE MAY NOT SURVIVE OUR JOURNEY HOME.
September 7th
WE ARE STILL SURROUNDED BY MOUNTAINS OF ICE. WE MUST TURN BACK.
WE WILL WAIT A FEW MORE DAYS. PERHAPS THE ICE WILL BREAK.
September 9th
I CANNOT LEAD THE MEN FURTHER INTO DANGER. WE MUST RETURN TO ENGLAND.
IF YOU WILL, BUT I WILL NOT. MY PURPOSE IS ASSIGNED TO ME BY HEAVEN.
I AM WEAK, BUT SURELY THE SPIRITS WHO ASSIST MY VENGEANCE WILL ENDOW ME WITH SUFFICIENT STRENGTH!

YOUR FRIEND HAS CERTAINLY NOT MANY HOURS TO LIVE.

I FEEL THAT I SHALL SOON DIE, WHILE *HE*, MY CREATION, MY ENEMY AND MY PERSECUTOR, *LIVES ON*.

THE TASK OF HIS DESTRUCTION WAS MINE, BUT I HAVE FAILED.

I ASK *YOU* NOW TO UNDERTAKE MY UNFINISHED WORK.

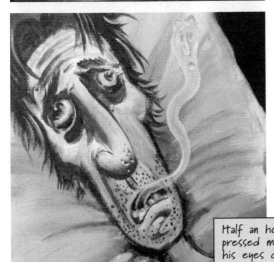

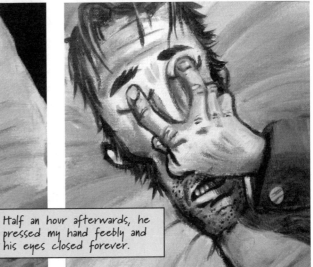

Half an hour afterwards, he pressed my hand feebly and his eyes closed forever.

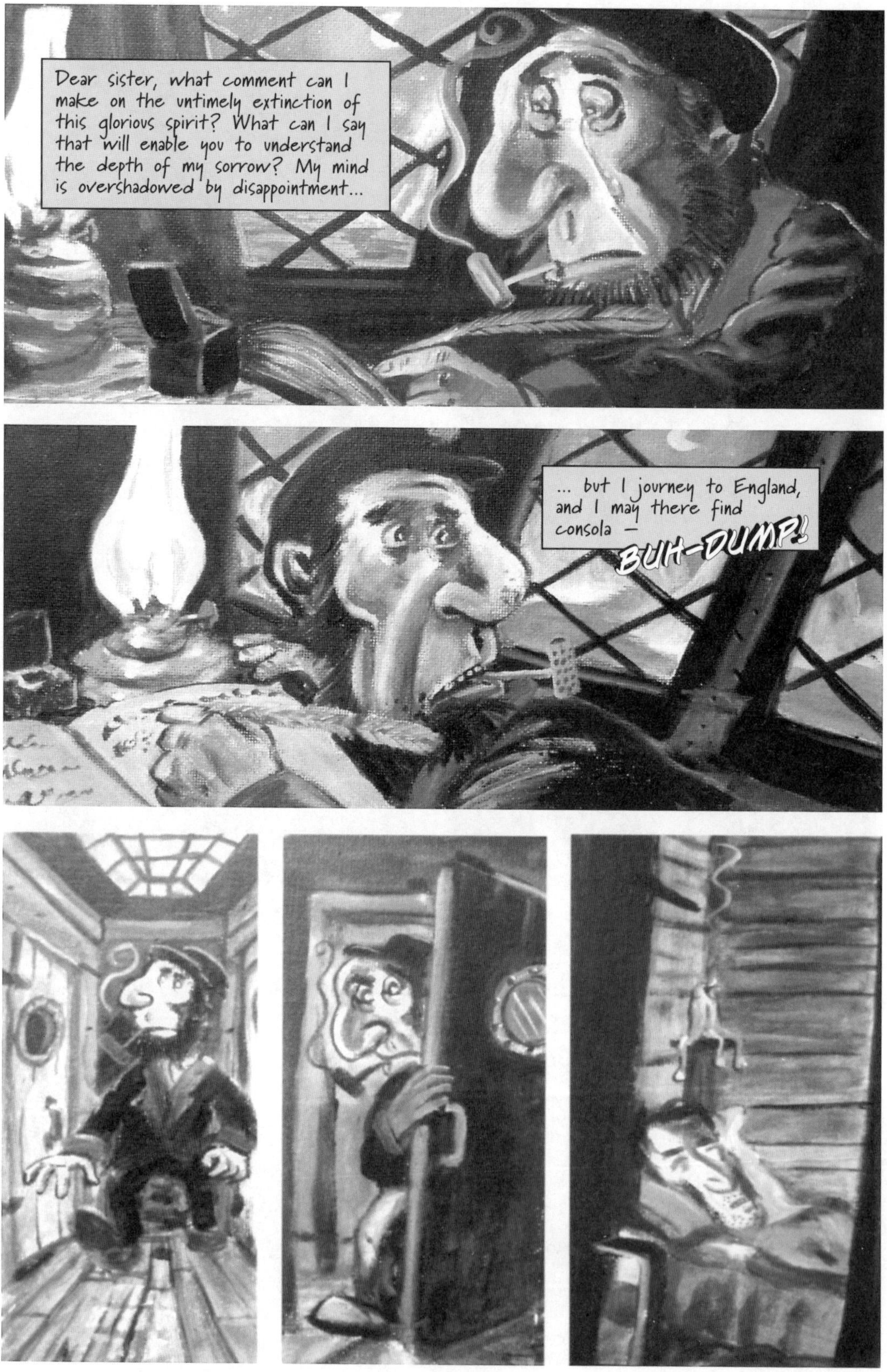
Dear sister, what comment can I make on the untimely extinction of this glorious spirit? What can I say that will enable you to understand the depth of my sorrow? My mind is overshadowed by disappointment...
... but I journey to England, and I may there find consola —
BUH-DUMP!

STAY!

THAT IS MY *FINAL VICTIM!* IN HIS MURDER, THE MISERABLE SERIES OF MY BEING IS WOUND TO ITS CLOSE!

FRANKENSTEIN, WHAT DOES IT AVAIL THAT I ASK THEE TO *PARDON* ME? I, WHO *DESTROYED* THEE BY DESTROYING ALL THOU LOVED!

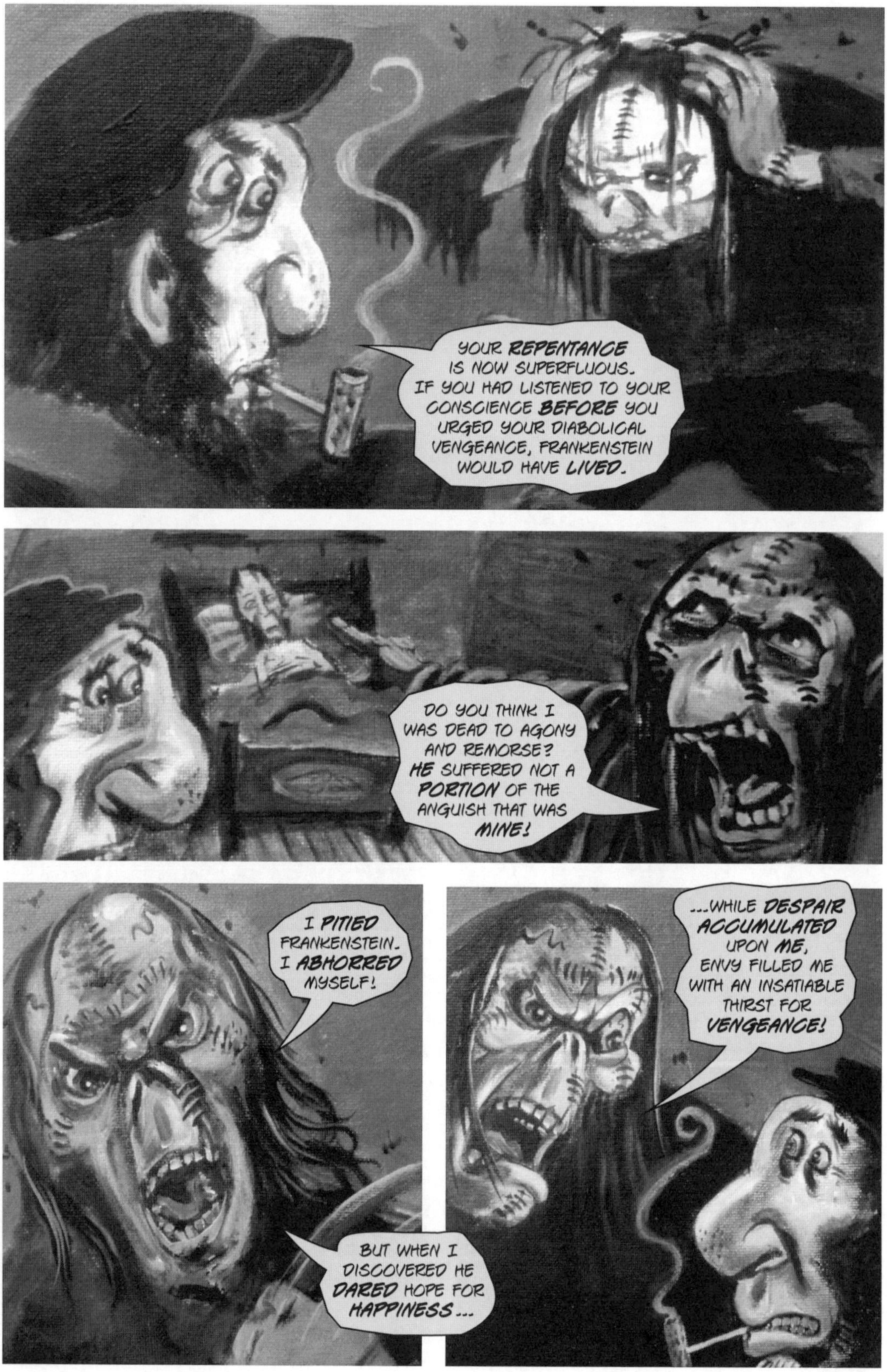
YOUR REPENTANCE IS NOW SUPERFLUOUS. IF YOU HAD LISTENED TO YOUR CONSCIENCE BEFORE YOU URGED YOUR DIABOLICAL VENGEANCE, FRANKENSTEIN WOULD HAVE LIVED.
DO YOU THINK I WAS DEAD TO AGONY AND REMORSE? HE SUFFERED NOT A PORTION OF THE ANGUISH THAT WAS MINE!
I PITIED FRANKENSTEIN. I ABHORRED MYSELF!
BUT WHEN I DISCOVERED HE DARED HOPE FOR HAPPINESS...
...WHILE DESPAIR ACCUMULATED UPON ME, ENVY FILLED ME WITH AN INSATIABLE THIRST FOR VENGEANCE!

AND NOW...
IT IS ENDED!

WRETCH!
HYPOCRITICAL FIEND!
YOU *LAMENT* ONLY
BECAUSE YOUR VICTIM
IS WITHDRAWN FROM
YOUR *POWER!*

OH, IT IS *NOT*
THUS. YET *I* SEEK
NOT A FELLOW
FEELING IN MY
MISERY. *I* AM
CONTENT TO
SUFFER *ALONE.*

FEAR NOT THAT I
SHALL BE THE INSTRUMENT
OF FUTURE MISCHIEF.
MY WORK IS NEARLY
COMPLETE.

I SHALL QUIT YOUR
VESSEL ON THE ICE RAFT WHICH
BROUGHT ME AND SEEK THE
MOST NORTHERN EXTREMITY OF
THE GLOBE.

THERE I SHALL COLLECT MY
FUNERAL PILE AND CONSUME TO ASHES
THIS MISERABLE FRAME.
I SHALL *DIE.*

FAREWELL!
SOON THESE
BURNING MISERIES
WILL BE *EXTINCT!*

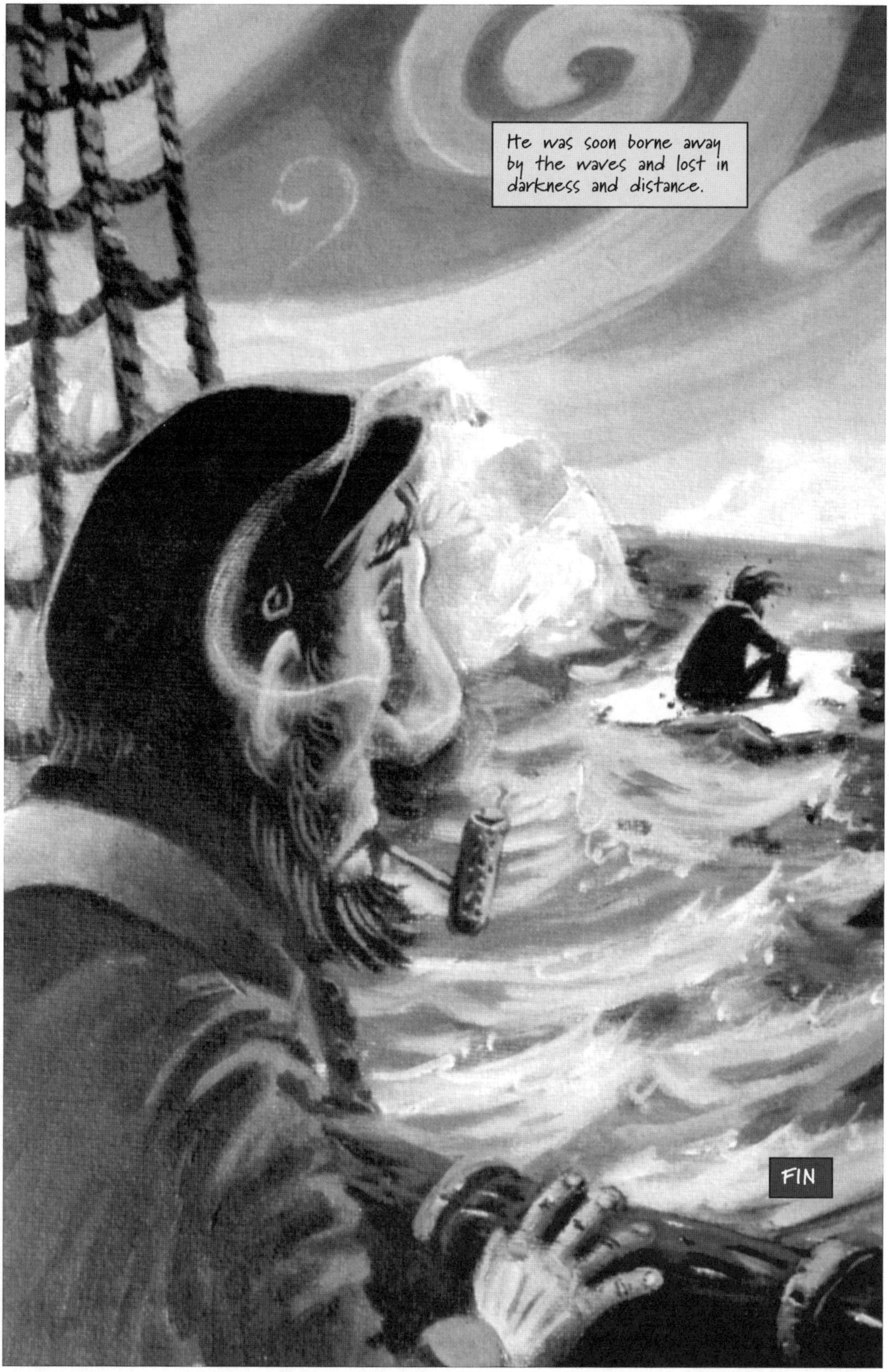
He was soon borne away by the waves and lost in darkness and distance.
FIN

Rappaccini's Daughter
BY NATHANIEL HAWTHORNE

ADAPTED BY
LANCE TOOKS

A YOUNG MAN NAMED GIOVANNI GUASCONTI CAME, VERY LONG AGO, FROM THE MORE SOUTHERN REGION OF ITALY TO PURSUE HIS STUDIES AT THE UNIVERSITY OF PADUA. GIOVANNI, WHO HAD BUT A SCANTY SUPPLY OF GOLD DUCATS IN HIS POCKET, TOOK LODGINGS IN A HIGH AND GLOOMY CHAMBER OF AN OLD EDIFICE.

OLD DAME LISABETTA, WON BY THE YOUTH'S REMARKABLE BEAUTY OF PERSON, ENDEAVORED TO GIVE THE CHAMBER A HABITABLE AIR. SHE GENTLY SUGGESTED HE LOOK OUT OF HIS BEDROOM WINDOW TO SEE SUNSHINE AS BRIGHT AS THAT HE LEFT BEHIND.

Does this garden belong to the house?

Heaven forbid, signor! That garden is cultivated by the own hands of Signor Giacomo Rappaccini, the famous Doctor, who has surely been heard of as far as Naples.

Rappaccini...

It is said he distils these plants into medicines that are as potent as a charm. Oftentimes you may see the Signor Doctor at work, and perchance the Signora his daughter, too, gathering the strange flowers that grow in the garden.

GIOVANNI FOUND NO BETTER OCCUPATION THAN TO LOOK DOWN INTO THE GARDEN BELOW. THERE WAS THE RUIN OF A MARBLE FOUNTAIN IN THE CENTER. A LITTLE GURGLING SOUND ASCENDED TO THE YOUNG MAN'S WINDOW, AND MADE HIM FEEL AS IF THE FOUNTAIN WERE AN IMMORTAL SPIRIT THAT SUNG WITHOUT HEEDING THE VICISSITUDES AROUND IT.

ALL ABOUT THE POOL INTO WHICH THE WATER SUBSIDED GREW VARIOUS PLANTS AND FLOWERS, GORGEOUSLY MAGNIFICENT. THERE WAS ONE SHRUB IN PARTICULAR, SET IN A MARBLE VASE IN THE MIDST OF THE POOL, THAT BORE A PROFUSION OF PURPLE BLOSSOMS; AND THE WHOLE TOGETHER MADE A SHOW SO RESPLENDENT THAT IT SEEMED ENOUGH TO ILLUMINATE THE GARDEN, EVEN HAD THERE BEEN NO SUNSHINE.

WHILE GIOVANNI STOOD AT THE WINDOW, HE HEARD A RUSTLING BEHIND A SCREEN OF LEAVES, AND BECAME AWARE THAT A PERSON WAS AT WORK IN THE GARDEN. HIS FIGURE SOON EMERGED INTO VIEW AND SHOWED ITSELF TO BE THAT OF NO COMMON LABORER, BUT A TALL, EMACIATED, SALLOW AND SICKLY LOOKING MAN, DRESSED IN A SCHOLAR'S GARB OF BLACK. HE WAS BEYOND THE MIDDLE TERM OF LIFE, WITH GRAY HAIR AND A FACE SINGULARLY MARKED WITH INTELLECT AND CULTIVATION, BUT WHICH COULD NEVER, EVEN IN HIS MORE YOUTHFUL DAYS, HAVE EXPRESSED MUCH WARMTH OF HEART.

NOTHING COULD EXCEED THE INTENTNESS WITH WHICH THIS SCIENTIFIC GARDENER EXAMINED EVERY SHRUB. NEVERTHELESS, THERE WAS NO APPROACH TO INTIMACY BETWEEN HIMSELF AND THESE VEGETABLE EXISTENCES. ON THE CONTRARY, HE AVOIDED THEIR ACTUAL TOUCH, OR THE DIRECT INHALING OF THEIR ODORS, WITH A DISAGREEABLE CAUTION. THE MAN'S DEMEANOR WAS THAT OF ONE WALKING AMONG MALIGNANT INFLUENCES, SUCH AS SAVAGE BEASTS OR DEADLY SNAKES WHICH, SHOULD HE ALLOW THEM ONE MOMENT OF LICENSE, WOULD WREAK UPON HIM SOME TERRIBLE FATALITY.

THE DISTRUSTFUL GARDENER DEFENDED HIS HANDS WITH A PAIR OF THICK GLOVES. WHEN, IN HIS WALK THROUGH THE GARDEN, HE CAME TO THE MAGNIFICENT PURPLE BLOSSOMS, HE PLACED A MASK OVER HIS MOUTH AND NOSTRILS, AS IF ALL THIS BEAUTY DID BUT CONCEAL A DEADLIER MALICE. BUT FINDING HIS TASK STILL TOO DANGEROUS, HE DREW BACK, REMOVED THE MASK, AND CALLED IN THE INFIRM VOICE OF A PERSON AFFECTED WITH DISEASE:

Beatrice! – Beatrice!

Here I am, my father!

Come, Beatrice, I need your help.

SOON THERE EMERGED THE FIGURE OF A YOUNG GIRL, ARRAYED WITH AS MUCH RICHNESS OF TASTE AS THE MOST SPLENDID OF THE FLOWERS; BEAUTIFUL AS THE DAY, AND WITH A BLOOM SO DEEP AND VIVID THAT ONE SHADE MORE WOULD HAVE BEEN TOO MUCH.

SHE LOOKED REDUNDANT WITH LIFE AND HEALTH.

YET GIOVANNI'S FANCY MUST HAVE GROWN MORBID WHILE HE LOOKED DOWN INTO THE GARDEN; IT WAS AS IF HERE WERE ANOTHER FLOWER, THE HUMAN SISTER OF THOSE VEGETABLE ONES, MORE BEAUTIFUL THAN THE RICHEST OF THEM — BUT STILL TO BE TOUCHED ONLY WITH A GLOVE, NOR TO BE APPROACHED WITHOUT A MASK. AS BEATRICE CAME DOWN THE GARDEN PATH SHE HANDLED AND INHALED THE ODOR OF SEVERAL OF THE PLANTS WHICH HER FATHER HAD MOST SEDULOUSLY AVOIDED.

SHE BENT TOWARDS THE MAGNIFICENT PLANT OF PURPLE BLOSSOMS, AND OPENED HER ARMS AS IF TO EMBRACE IT.

Yes, my sister, it shall be Beatrice's task to serve thee; and thou shalt reward her with thy kisses and perfume breath, which to her is as the breath of life!

DOCTOR RAPPACCINI HAD FINISHED HIS LABORS IN THE GARDEN, AND HE NOW TOOK HIS DAUGHTER'S ARM AND RETIRED. NIGHT WAS ALREADY CLOSING IN, AND GIOVANNI WENT TO HIS COUCH AND DREAMED OF A RICH FLOWER AND BEAUTIFUL GIRL. FLOWER AND MAIDEN WERE DIFFERENT AND YET THE SAME, AND FRAUGHT WITH SOME STRANGE PERIL IN EITHER SHAPE.

THE NEXT DAY HE PAID HIS RESPECTS TO SIGNOR PIETRO BAGLIONI, PROFESSOR OF MEDICINE IN THE UNIVERSITY, A PHYSICIAN OF EMINENT REPUTE, TO WHOM GIOVANNI HAD BROUGHT A LETTER OF INTRODUCTION. GIOVANNI TOOK AN OPPORTUNITY TO MENTION THE NAME OF DOCTOR RAPPACCINI. BUT THE PROFESSOR DID NOT RESPOND WITH SO MUCH CORDIALITY AS HE HAD ANTICIPATED.

Rappaccini cares infinitely more for science than for mankind. His patients are interesting to him only as subjects for experiment. He would sacrifice life, or whatever was dearest to him, for the sake of a grain of knowledge.

Now and then, it must be owned, he has effected a marvelous cure. But he should receive little credit for such instances of success — they being probably the work of chance — but should be held strictly accountable for his failures, which may justly be considered his own work.

You have heard, no doubt, of his daughter, whom all the young men in Padua are wild about, though not half a dozen have ever seen her face.

I know little of the Signora Beatrice, save that Rappaccini is said to have instructed her deeply in his science, and that, young and beautiful as fame reports her, she is already qualified to fill a professor's chair. Perchance her father destines her for mine!

THE YOUTH MIGHT HAVE TAKEN BAGLIONI'S OPINIONS WITH SOME ALLOWANCE, HAD HE KNOWN THAT THERE WAS A PROFESSIONAL WARFARE OF LONG CONTINUANCE BETWEEN HIM AND DOCTOR RAPPACCINI, IN WHICH THE LATTER WAS THOUGHT TO HAVE GAINED THE ADVANTAGE.

GIOVANNI RETURNED TO HIS LODGINGS, HIS BRAIN SWIMMING. ON HIS WAY, HAPPENING TO PASS BY A FLORIST'S, HE BOUGHT A FRESH BOUQUET. ASCENDING TO HIS CHAMBER, HE SEATED HIMSELF NEAR THE WINDOW, CONCEALED IN SHADOW. AT FIRST THE GARDEN WAS A SOLITUDE. SOON, HOWEVER, A FIGURE APPEARED BENEATH THE ANTIQUE PORTAL. ON AGAIN BEHOLDING BEATRICE, THE YOUNG MAN WAS STRUCK ONCE MORE BY HER BEAUTY AND HER EXPRESSION OF SIMPLICITY AND SWEETNESS, WHICH MADE HIM ASK ANEW WHAT MANNER OF MORTAL SHE MIGHT BE.

NOR DID HE FAIL AGAIN TO OBSERVE AN ANALOGY BETWEEN THE BEAUTIFUL GIRL AND THE SHRUB THAT HUNG OVER THE FOUNTAIN; A RESEMBLANCE WHICH BEATRICE INDULGED BY THE ARRANGEMENT OF HER DRESS AND THE SELECTION OF ITS HUES.

Give me thy breath, my sister, for I am faint with common air! And give me this flower of thine, which I separate with gentlest fingers from the stem, and place close beside my heart.

WITH THESE WORDS, THE BEAUTIFUL DAUGHTER OF RAPPACCINI PLUCKED ONE OF THE RICHEST BLOSSOMS OF THE SHRUB, AND WAS ABOUT TO FASTEN IT IN HER BOSOM. BUT NOW A SINGULAR INCIDENT OCCURRED: A SMALL REPTILE SCURRIED AT HER FEET, AND A DROP OF MOISTURE FROM THE BROKEN STEM OF THE FLOWER FELL BY CHANCE UPON THE LIZARD'S HEAD.

FOR AN INSTANT, THE REPTILE CONTORTED ITSELF VIOLENTLY, AND THEN LAY MOTIONLESS. BEATRICE CROSSED HERSELF, SADLY, BUT WITHOUT SURPRISE; NOR DID SHE HESITATE TO ARRANGE THE FATAL FLOWER IN HER BOSOM. GIOVANNI, OUT OF THE SHADOW OF HIS WINDOW, BENT FORWARD AND TREMBLED.

What is this being? Beautiful – or inexpressibly terrible?

AT THIS MOMENT, THERE CAME A BEAUTIFUL INSECT OVER THE GARDEN WALL, LURED FROM AFAR BY THE HEAVY PERFUMES OF DOCTOR RAPPACCINI'S SHRUBS. IT SEEMED TO BE ATTRACTED BY BEATRICE, AND FLUTTERED ABOUT HER HEAD. THEN, WHILE BEATRICE WAS GAZING AT THE INSECT WITH CHILDISH DELIGHT, IT GREW FAINT AND FELL LIFELESS AT HER FEET; FROM NO CAUSE GIOVANNI COULD DISCERN, UNLESS IT WERE THE ATMOSPHERE OF HER BREATH.

AN IMPULSIVE MOVEMENT OF GIOVANNI DREW HER EYES TO THE WINDOW. THERE SHE BEHELD THE BEAUTIFUL HEAD OF THE YOUNG MAN GAZING DOWN UPON HER LIKE A BEING THAT HOVERED IN MID-AIR. SCARCELY KNOWING WHAT HE DID, GIOVANNI THREW DOWN THE BOUQUET.

Signora, here are pure and healthful flowers. Wear them for the sake of Giovanni Guasconti!

I accept your gift, and would fain recompense it with this precious purple flower; but if I toss it into the air, it will not reach you. So Signor Guasconti must content himself with my thanks.

SHE REPLIED WITH A RICH VOICE THAT CAME FORTH AS IT WERE A GUSH OF MUSIC, AND WITH A MIRTHFUL EXPRESSION HALF CHILDISH AND HALF WOMAN-LIKE.

SHE LIFTED THE BOUQUET TO HER BREAST, AND THEN, AS IF INWARDLY ASHAMED AT HAVING STEPPED ASIDE FROM HER MAIDENLY RESERVE TO RESPOND TO A STRANGER'S GREETING, PASSED SWIFTLY HOMEWARD THROUGH THE GARDEN. BUT, FEW AS THE MOMENTS WERE, IT SEEMED TO GIOVANNI THAT WHEN SHE WAS ON THE POINT OF VANISHING BENEATH THE SCULPTURED PORTAL, HIS BEAUTIFUL BOUQUET WAS ALREADY BEGINNING TO WITHER IN HER GRASP.

FOR MANY DAYS THE YOUNG MAN AVOIDED THE WINDOW THAT LOOKED INTO DOCTOR RAPPACCINI'S GARDEN, AS IF SOMETHING MONSTROUS WOULD HAVE BLASTED HIS SIGHT. HE FELT CONSCIOUS OF HAVING PUT HIMSELF WITHIN THE INFLUENCE OF AN UNINTELLIGIBLE POWER, BY THE COMMUNICATION WHICH HE HAD OPENED WITH BEATRICE. THE WISEST COURSE WOULD HAVE BEEN TO QUIT HIS LODGINGS, AND PADUA ITSELF, AT ONCE.

WHETHER OR NOT BEATRICE POSSESSED THOSE TERRIBLE ATTRIBUTES — THAT FATAL BREATH — THE AFFINITY WITH THOSE DEADLY FLOWERS — SHE HAD INSTILLED A SUBTLE POISON INTO HIS SYSTEM. IT WAS NOT LOVE, NOR HORROR, BUT A WILD OFFSPRING OF BOTH THAT BURNED LIKE ONE AND SHIVERED LIKE THE OTHER. HOPE AND DREAD KEPT A CONTINUAL WARFARE IN HIM, ALTERNATELY VANQUISHING ONE ANOTHER, THEN STARTING UP AFRESH TO RENEW THE CONTEST.

SOMETIMES GIOVANNI ENDEAVORED TO ASSUAGE THE FEVER OF HIS SPIRIT BY A RAPID WALK THROUGH THE STREETS OF PADUA. ONE DAY HE FOUND HIS ARM SEIZED BY A PORTLY PERSONAGE WHO HAD EXPENDED MUCH BREATH IN OVERTAKING HIM.

Signor Giovanni! Have you forgotten me? That might well be the case, if I were as much altered as yourself.

Yes: I am Giovanni Guasconti. You are Professor Pietro Baglioni. Now let me pass!

WHILE THEY WERE SPEAKING, THERE CAME A MAN IN BLACK ALONG THE STREET. HIS FACE WAS OVERSPREAD WITH A MOST SICKLY AND SALLOW HUE, BUT YET SO PERVADED WITH AN EXPRESSION OF PIERCING AND ACTIVE INTELLECT THAT AN OBSERVER MIGHT EASILY HAVE SEEN ONLY HIS WONDERFUL ENERGY. AS HE PASSED, THIS PERSON EXCHANGED A COLD AND DISTANT SALUTATION WITH BAGLIONI, BUT FIXED HIS EYES UPON GIOVANNI WITH AN INTENTNESS THAT SEEMED TO BRING OUT WHATEVER WAS WITHIN HIM WORTHY OF NOTICE. THERE WAS A PECULIAR QUIETNESS IN THE LOOK, AS IF TAKING MERELY A SPECULATIVE, NOT A HUMAN INTEREST, IN THE YOUNG MAN.

It is Doctor Rappaccini! For some purpose or other, this man of science is making a study of you! I know that look of his! It is the same that coldly illuminates his face as he bends over a bird, a mouse, or a butterfly, which, in pursuance of some experiment, he has killed by the perfume of a flower – a look as deep as Nature itself, but without Nature's warmth of love. Signor Giovanni, I will stake my life upon it – you are the subject of one of Rappaccini's experiments!

GIOVANNI, FINDING BAGLIONI'S PERTINACITY INTOLERABLE, BROKE AWAY, AND WAS GONE BEFORE THE PROFESSOR COULD AGAIN SEIZE HIS ARM. ON RETURNING TO HIS LODGINGS, HE WAS MET BY OLD LISABETTA.

IT CROSSED HIS MIND THAT THIS INTERPOSITION OF LISABETTA MIGHT BE CONNECTED WITH THE INTRIGUE IN WHICH THE PROFESSOR CLAIMED THAT DOCTOR RAPPACCINI WAS INVOLVING HIM. BUT THE SUSPICION WAS INADEQUATE TO RESTRAIN HIM. THE INSTANT HE WAS AWARE OF THE POSSIBILITY OF APPROACHING BEATRICE, IT SEEMED AN ABSOLUTE NECESSITY OF HIS EXISTENCE TO DO SO. IT MATTERED NOT WHETHER SHE WERE ANGEL OR DEMON.

Listen, Signor! There is a private entrance into the garden...

Show me the way!

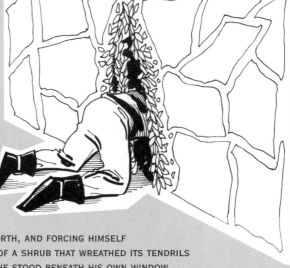

HIS WITHERED GUIDE LED HIM ALONG OBSCURE PASSAGES, AND FINALLY UNDID A DOOR. GIOVANNI STEPPED FORTH, AND FORCING HIMSELF THROUGH THE ENTANGLEMENT OF A SHRUB THAT WREATHED ITS TENDRILS OVER THE HIDDEN ENTRANCE, HE STOOD BENEATH HIS OWN WINDOW, IN THE OPEN AREA OF DOCTOR RAPPACCINI'S GARDEN.

PERCEIVING THAT HE WAS ALONE, HE BEGAN A CRITICAL OBSERVATION OF THE PLANTS. THERE WAS HARDLY AN INDIVIDUAL SHRUB WHICH A WANDERER, STRAYING BY HIMSELF THROUGH A FOREST, WOULD NOT HAVE BEEN STARTLED TO FIND GROWING WILD, AS IF AN UNEARTHLY FACE HAD GLARED AT HIM OUT OF THE THICKET. THEIR PRODUCTION SEEMED NOT OF GOD'S MAKING, BUT THE MONSTROUS OFFSPRING OF MAN'S DEPRAVED FANCY, GLOWING WITH ONLY AN EVIL MOCKERY OF BEAUTY. GIOVANNI RECOGNIZED BUT TWO OR THREE PLANTS IN THE COLLECTION, AND THOSE OF A KIND THAT HE WELL KNEW TO BE POISONOUS. THEN SUDDENLY HE HEARD THE RUSTLING OF A SILKEN GARMENT, AND TURNING, BEHELD BEATRICE EMERGING FROM BENEATH THE SCULPTURED PORTAL.

GIOVANNI HAD NOT CONSIDERED WHAT SHOULD BE HIS DEPORTMENT, BUT BEATRICE'S MANNER PLACED HIM AT HIS EASE. SHE CAME LIGHTLY ALONG THE PATH AND MET HIM NEAR THE FOUNTAIN. THERE WAS SURPRISE IN HER FACE, BUT BRIGHTENED BY A SIMPLE AND KIND EXPRESSION OF PLEASURE.

You are a connoisseur in flowers. If my father were here, he could tell you many interesting facts as to the nature and habits of these shrubs, for this garden is his world.

Would you deign to be my instructress?... And must I believe all that I have seen with my own eyes? Bid me believe nothing, save what comes from your lips.

Forget whatever you may have fancied in regard to me. If true to the outward senses, still it may be false in essence. But the words of Beatrice Rappaccini's lips are true from the heart outward. Those you may believe!

A FERVOR GLOWED IN HER WHOLE ASPECT, AND BEAMED UPON GIOVANNI'S CONSCIOUSNESS LIKE THE LIGHT OF TRUTH ITSELF. BUT YET THERE WAS A FRAGRANCE IN THE ATMOSPHERE AROUND HER WHICH THE YOUNG MAN SCARCELY DARED TO DRAW INTO HIS LUNGS. IT MIGHT BE THE ODOR OF THE FLOWERS. OR COULD IT BE BEATRICE'S BREATH WHICH EMBALMED HER WORDS WITH A STRANGE RICHNESS?

A FAINTNESS PASSED LIKE A SHADOW OVER HIM AND FLITTED AWAY; HE SEEMED TO GAZE THROUGH THE BEAUTIFUL GIRL'S EYES INTO HER TRANSPARENT SOUL, AND FELT NO MORE DOUBT OR FEAR.

THE TINGE OF PASSION THAT HAD COLORED BEATRICE'S MANNER VANISHED; SHE BECAME GAY, AND APPEARED TO DERIVE A PURE DELIGHT FROM HER COMMUNION WITH THE YOUTH, NOT UNLIKE WHAT THE MAIDEN OF A LONELY ISLAND MIGHT HAVE FELT CONVERSING WITH A VOYAGER FROM THE CIVILIZED WORLD. EVIDENTLY HER EXPERIENCE OF LIFE HAD BEEN CONFINED WITHIN THE LIMITS OF THAT GARDEN. SHE TALKED NOW ABOUT MATTERS AS SIMPLE AS THE DAYLIGHT OR SUMMER CLOUDS, AND ASKED QUESTIONS IN REFERENCE TO THE CITY, OR GIOVANNI'S HOME, HIS FRIENDS, HIS MOTHER, AND HIS SISTERS; QUESTIONS INDICATING SUCH SECLUSION, AND LACK OF FAMILIARITY WITH MODES AND FORMS, THAT GIOVANNI RESPONDED AS IF TO AN INFANT.

EVER AND ANON, THERE GLEAMED ACROSS THE YOUNG MAN'S MIND A SENSE OF WONDER, THAT HE SHOULD BE WALKING SIDE BY SIDE WITH THE BEING WHO HAD SO WROUGHT UPON HIS IMAGINATION — WHOM HE HAD IDEALIZED IN SUCH HUES OF TERROR — IN WHOM HE HAD POSITIVELY WITNESSED SUCH MANIFESTATIONS OF DREADFUL ATTRIBUTES — THAT HE SHOULD BE CONVERSING WITH BEATRICE LIKE A BROTHER, AND SHOULD FIND HER SO HUMAN AND SO MAIDEN-LIKE. BUT SUCH REFLECTIONS WERE ONLY MOMENTARY; THE EFFECT OF HER CHARACTER WAS TOO REAL NOT TO MAKE ITSELF FAMILIAR AT ONCE.

AFTER MANY TURNS AMONG THE GARDEN'S AVENUES, THEY CAME TO THE FOUNTAIN, BESIDE WHICH GREW THE MAGNIFICENT SHRUB WITH ITS GLOWING BLOSSOMS. A FRAGRANCE WAS DIFFUSED FROM IT, WHICH GIOVANNI RECOGNIZED AS IDENTICAL WITH THAT WHICH HE HAD ATTRIBUTED TO BEATRICE'S BREATH, BUT INCOMPARABLY MORE POWERFUL. AS HER EYES FELL UPON IT, SHE PRESSED HER HAND TO HER BOSOM.

For the first time in my life, I had forgotten thee!

I remember, Signora, that you once promised to reward me with one of these living gems for the bouquet which I had the happy boldness to fling to your feet. Permit me now to pluck it as a memorial of this interview.

HE MADE A STEP TOWARDS THE SHRUB WITH EXTENDED HAND. BUT BEATRICE DARTED FORWARD, UTTERING A SHRIEK THAT WENT THROUGH HIS HEART LIKE A DAGGER.

SHE CAUGHT HIS HAND, AND DREW IT BACK WITH THE WHOLE FORCE OF HER SLENDER FIGURE. GIOVANNI FELT HER TOUCH THRILLING THROUGH HIS FIBRES.

Touch it not! Not for thy life! It is fatal!

THEN, HIDING HER FACE, SHE FLED FROM HIM AND VANISHED BENEATH THE SCULPTURED PORTAL.

AS GIOVANNI FOLLOWED HER WITH HIS EYES, HE BEHELD THE EMACIATED FIGURE AND PALE INTELLIGENCE OF DOCTOR RAPPACCINI, WHO HAD BEEN WATCHING THE SCENE, HE KNEW NOT HOW LONG, FROM WITHIN THE SHADOW OF THE ENTRANCE.

NO SOONER WAS GIOVANNI ALONE IN HIS CHAMBER, THAN THE IMAGE OF BEATRICE CAME BACK TO HIS PASSIONATE MUSINGS, INVESTED WITH ALL THE WITCHERY THAT HAD BEEN GATHERING AROUND IT EVER SINCE HIS FIRST GLIMPSE OF HER, AND NOW LIKEWISE IMBUED WITH A TENDER WARMTH OF GIRLISH WOMANHOOD. THUS DID GIOVANNI SPEND THE NIGHT, UNTIL THE DAWN HAD BEGUN TO AWAKE THE SLUMBERING FLOWERS IN DOCTOR RAPPACCINI'S GARDEN. THE SUN AWOKE HIM TO A SENSE OF PAIN. WHEN THOROUGHLY AROUSED, HE BECAME SENSIBLE OF A BURNING AND TINGLING AGONY IN HIS HAND — THE VERY HAND WHICH BEATRICE HAD GRASPED IN HER OWN WHEN HE WAS ON THE POINT OF PLUCKING ONE OF THE GEM-LIKE FLOWERS. ON THAT HAND THERE WAS NOW A PURPLE PRINT, LIKE THAT OF FOUR SMALL FINGERS AND A SLENDER THUMB.

GIOVANNI WRAPPED A HANDKERCHIEF ABOUT HIS HAND, WONDERED WHAT EVIL THING HAD STUNG HIM, AND SOON FORGOT HIS PAIN IN A REVERIE OF BEATRICE.

Oh, how stubbornly does love hold its faith, until the moment come, when it is doomed to vanish into thin mist!

A MEETING WITH BEATRICE IN THE GARDEN WAS NO LONGER AN INCIDENT IN GIOVANNI'S DAILY LIFE, BUT THE WHOLE SPACE IN WHICH HE MIGHT BE SAID TO LIVE; FOR THE ANTICIPATION AND MEMORY OF THAT ECSTATIC HOUR MADE UP THE REMAINDER. NOR WAS IT OTHERWISE WITH THE DAUGHTER OF RAPPACCINI. SHE WATCHED FOR THE YOUTH'S APPEARANCE, AND FLEW TO HIS SIDE WITH CONFIDENCE AS UNRESERVED AS IF THEY HAD BEEN PLAYMATES FROM INFANCY.

BUT WITH ALL THIS FAMILIARITY, THERE WAS STILL A RESERVE IN BEATRICE'S DEMEANOR, SO RIGIDLY AND INVARIABLY SUSTAINED, THAT THE IDEA OF INFRINGING IT SCARCELY OCCURRED TO HIS IMAGINATION. BY ALL APPRECIABLE SIGNS, THEY LOVED WITH EYES THAT CONVEYED THE HOLY SECRET FROM THE DEPTHS OF ONE SOUL INTO THE OTHER; AND YET THERE HAD BEEN NO SEAL OF LIPS, NO CLASP OF HANDS, NOR ANY SLIGHTEST CARESS, SUCH AS LOVE CLAIMS AND HALLOWS.

ONE MORNING GIOVANNI WAS DISAGREEABLY SURPRISED BY A VISIT FROM PROFESSOR BAGLIONI.

I have been reading an interesting story. It is of an Indian prince, who sent a beautiful woman as a present to Alexander the Great. She was lovely as the dawn, but what especially distinguished her was the rich perfume in her breath — richer than a garden of Persian roses. Alexander fell in love at first sight with this magnificent stranger. But a sage physician discovered a terrible secret in regard to her — this lovely woman had been nourished with poisons from her birth upward, until her whole nature was so imbued with them that she herself had become the deadliest poison in existence. Her love would have been poison: her embrace death!
Is not this a marvelous tale?

A childish fable.

My poor Giovanni! I know this wretched girl far better than yourself. That old Indian fable has become a truth, by the deadly science of Rappaccini, and in the person of the lovely Beatrice! Her father was not restrained by natural affection from offering up his child in this horrible manner as the victim of his insane zeal for science. What, then, will be your fate? Beyond a doubt, you are selected as the material of some new experiment. Perhaps the result is to be death — perhaps a fate more awful still!

GIOVANNI GROANED AND HID HIS FACE.

But be of good cheer, son of my friend! It is not yet too late for the rescue. Possibly, we may even succeed in bringing back this miserable child within the limits of ordinary nature, from which her father's madness has estranged her. Behold this little silver vase!
One sip of this antidote would have rendered the most virulent poisons of the Borgias innocuous. Doubt not that it will be as efficacious against those of Rappaccini. Bestow the precious liquid upon your Beatrice, and hopefully await the result.

ALONE ONCE MORE, HE RESOLVED TO INSTITUTE SOME DECISIVE TEST THAT SHOULD SATISFY HIM, ONCE AND FOR ALL, WHETHER THERE WERE THOSE DREADFUL PECULIARITIES IN HER PHYSICAL NATURE WHICH COULD NOT BE SUPPOSED TO EXIST WITHOUT SOME CORRESPONDING MONSTROSITY OF SOUL. HIS EYES, GAZING DOWN AFAR, MIGHT HAVE DECEIVED HIM AS TO THE LIZARD, THE INSECT, AND THE FLOWERS. BUT IF HE COULD WITNESS, AT THE DISTANCE OF A FEW PACES, THE SUDDEN BLIGHT OF ONE FRESH AND HEALTHFUL FLOWER IN BEATRICE'S HAND, THERE WOULD BE ROOM FOR NO FURTHER QUESTION. WITH THIS IDEA, HE HASTENED TO THE FLORIST'S, AND PURCHASED A BOUQUET THAT WAS STILL GEMMED WITH THE MORNING DEW-DROPS.

IT WAS NOW THE CUSTOMARY HOUR OF HIS DAILY INTERVIEW WITH BEATRICE. BEFORE DESCENDING INTO THE GARDEN, GIOVANNI FAILED NOT TO LOOK AT HIS FIGURE IN THE MIRROR; A VANITY TO BE EXPECTED IN A BEAUTIFUL YOUNG MAN, YET, AS DISPLAYING ITSELF AT THAT TROUBLED AND FEVERISH MOMENT, THE TOKEN OF A CERTAIN SHALLOWNESS OF CHARACTER. HE DID GAZE, HOWEVER, AND SAID TO HIMSELF THAT HIS FEATURES HAD NEVER BEFORE POSSESSED SO RICH A GRACE, NOR HIS EYES SUCH VIVACITY, NOR HIS CHEEKS SO WARM A HUE OF SUPERABUNDANT LIFE.

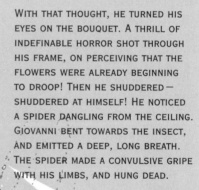

At least her poison has not yet insinuated itself into my system. I am no flower to perish in her grasp!

WITH THAT THOUGHT, HE TURNED HIS EYES ON THE BOUQUET. A THRILL OF INDEFINABLE HORROR SHOT THROUGH HIS FRAME, ON PERCEIVING THAT THE FLOWERS WERE ALREADY BEGINNING TO DROOP! THEN HE SHUDDERED — SHUDDERED AT HIMSELF! HE NOTICED A SPIDER DANGLING FROM THE CEILING. GIOVANNI BENT TOWARDS THE INSECT, AND EMITTED A DEEP, LONG BREATH. THE SPIDER MADE A CONVULSIVE GRIPE WITH HIS LIMBS, AND HUNG DEAD.

Accursed! Accursed! Hast thou grown so poisonous that this deadly insect perishes by thy breath?

AT THAT MOMENT, A RICH, SWEET VOICE CAME FLOATING UP FROM THE GARDEN:

Giovanni! Giovanni! It is past the hour! Come down!

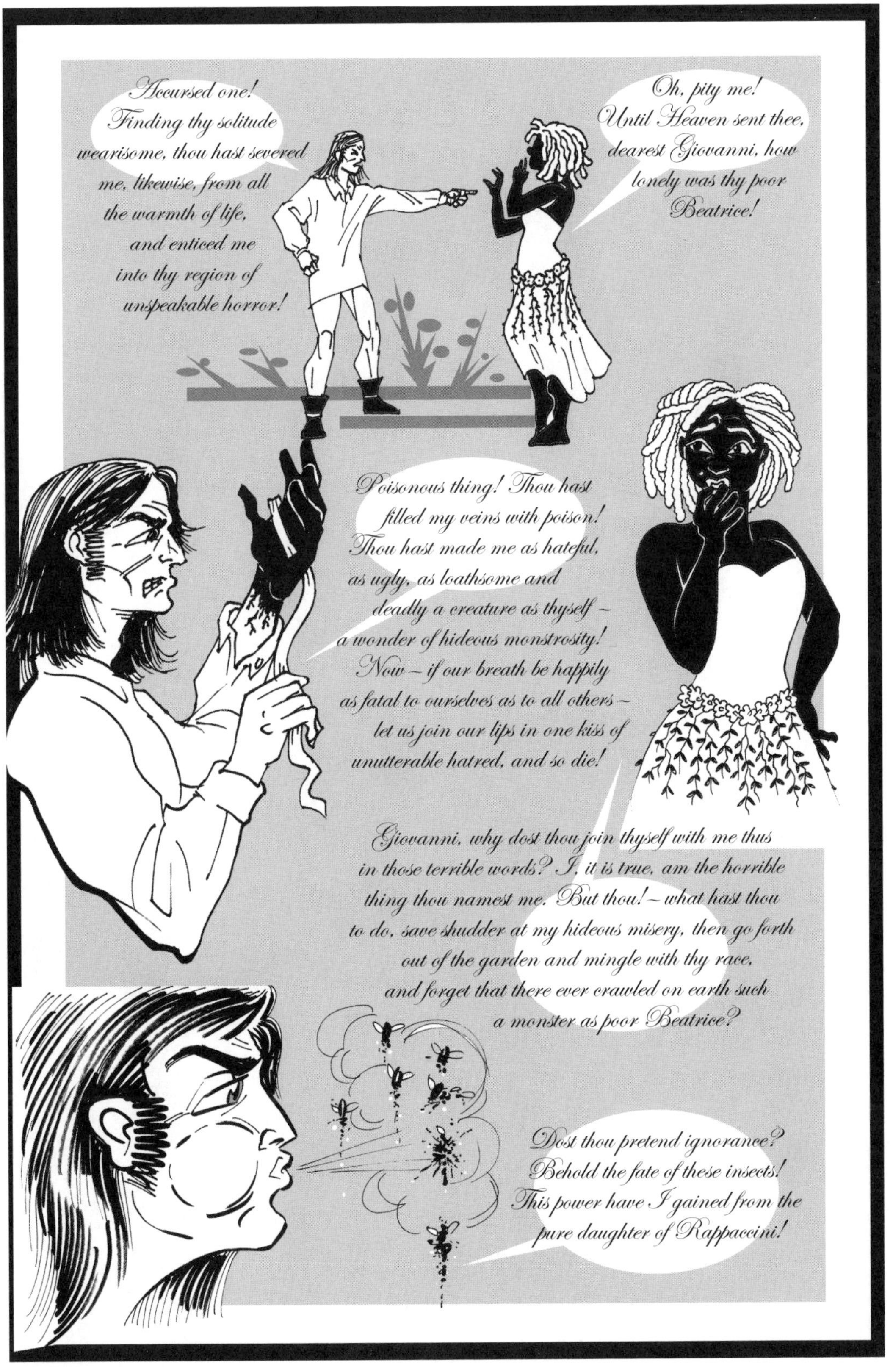
Accursed one! Finding thy solitude wearisome, thou hast severed me, likewise, from all the warmth of life, and enticed me into thy region of unspeakable horror!
Oh, pity me! Until Heaven sent thee, dearest Giovanni, how lonely was thy poor Beatrice!
Poisonous thing! Thou hast filled my veins with poison! Thou hast made me as hateful, as ugly, as loathsome and deadly a creature as thyself – a wonder of hideous monstrosity! Now – if our breath be happily as fatal to ourselves as to all others – let us join our lips in one kiss of unutterable hatred, and so die!
Giovanni, why dost thou join thyself with me thus in those terrible words? I, it is true, am the horrible thing thou namest me. But thou! – what hast thou to do, save shudder at my hideous misery, then go forth out of the garden and mingle with thy race, and forget that there ever crawled on earth such a monster as poor Beatrice?
Dost thou pretend ignorance? Behold the fate of these insects! This power have I gained from the pure daughter of Rappaccini!

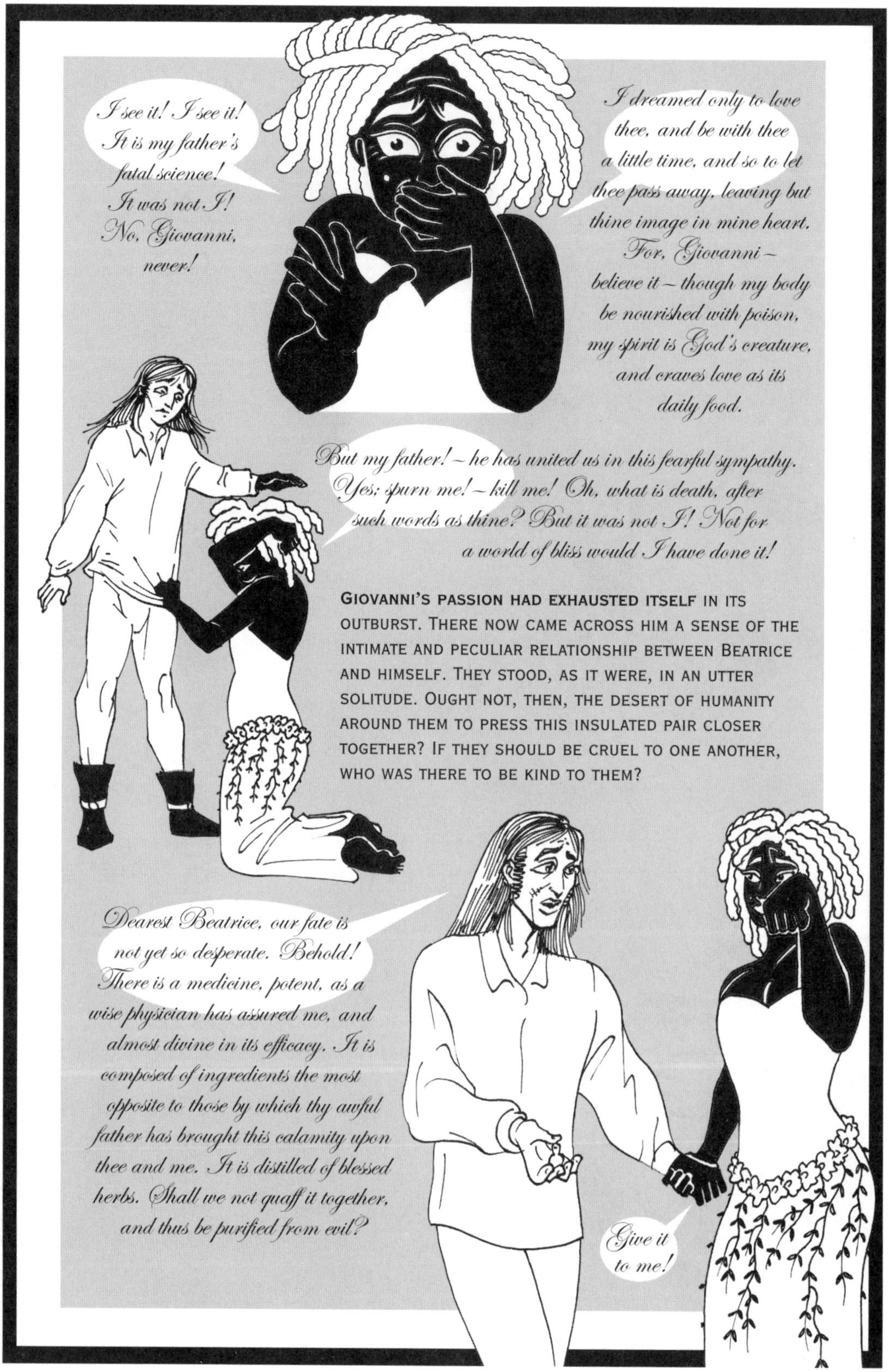
I see it! I see it! It is my father's fatal science! It was not I! No, Giovanni, never!
I dreamed only to love thee, and be with thee a little time, and so to let thee pass away, leaving but thine image in mine heart. For, Giovanni – believe it – though my body be nourished with poison, my spirit is God's creature, and craves love as its daily food.
But my father! – he has united us in this fearful sympathy. Yes; spurn me! – kill me! Oh, what is death, after such words as thine? But it was not I! Not for a world of bliss would I have done it!
GIOVANNI'S PASSION HAD EXHAUSTED ITSELF IN ITS OUTBURST. THERE NOW CAME ACROSS HIM A SENSE OF THE INTIMATE AND PECULIAR RELATIONSHIP BETWEEN BEATRICE AND HIMSELF. THEY STOOD, AS IT WERE, IN AN UTTER SOLITUDE. OUGHT NOT, THEN, THE DESERT OF HUMANITY AROUND THEM TO PRESS THIS INSULATED PAIR CLOSER TOGETHER? IF THEY SHOULD BE CRUEL TO ONE ANOTHER, WHO WAS THERE TO BE KIND TO THEM?
Dearest Beatrice, our fate is not yet so desperate. Behold! There is a medicine, potent, as a wise physician has assured me, and almost divine in its efficacy. It is composed of ingredients the most opposite to those by which thy awful father has brought this calamity upon thee and me. It is distilled of blessed herbs. Shall we not quaff it together, and thus be purified from evil?
Give it to me!

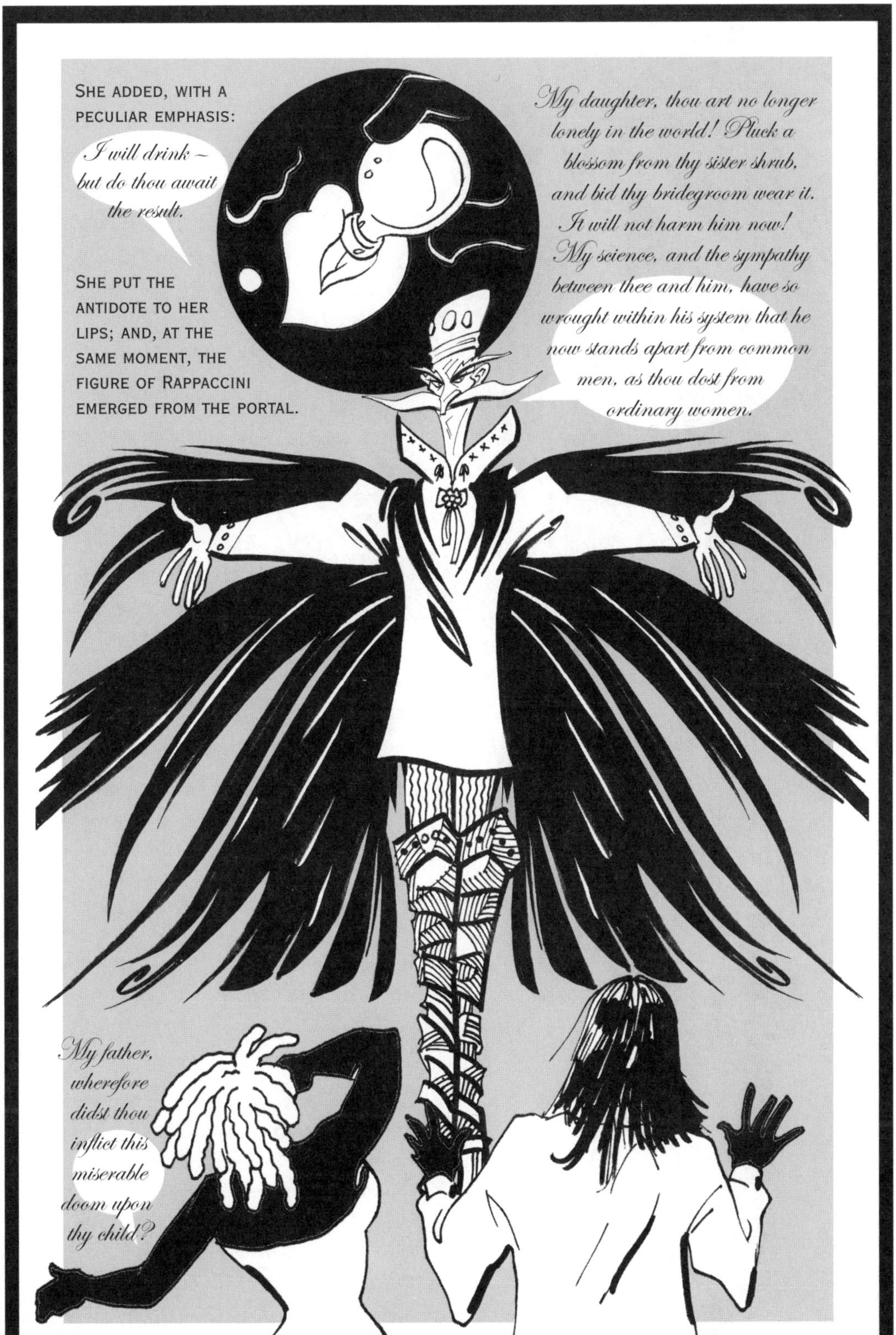
SHE ADDED, WITH A PECULIAR EMPHASIS:
I will drink—but do thou await the result.
SHE PUT THE ANTIDOTE TO HER LIPS; AND, AT THE SAME MOMENT, THE FIGURE OF RAPPACCINI EMERGED FROM THE PORTAL.
My daughter, thou art no longer lonely in the world! Pluck a blossom from thy sister shrub, and bid thy bridegroom wear it. It will not harm him now! My science, and the sympathy between thee and him, have so wrought within his system that he now stands apart from common men, as thou dost from ordinary women.
My father, wherefore didst thou inflict this miserable doom upon thy child?

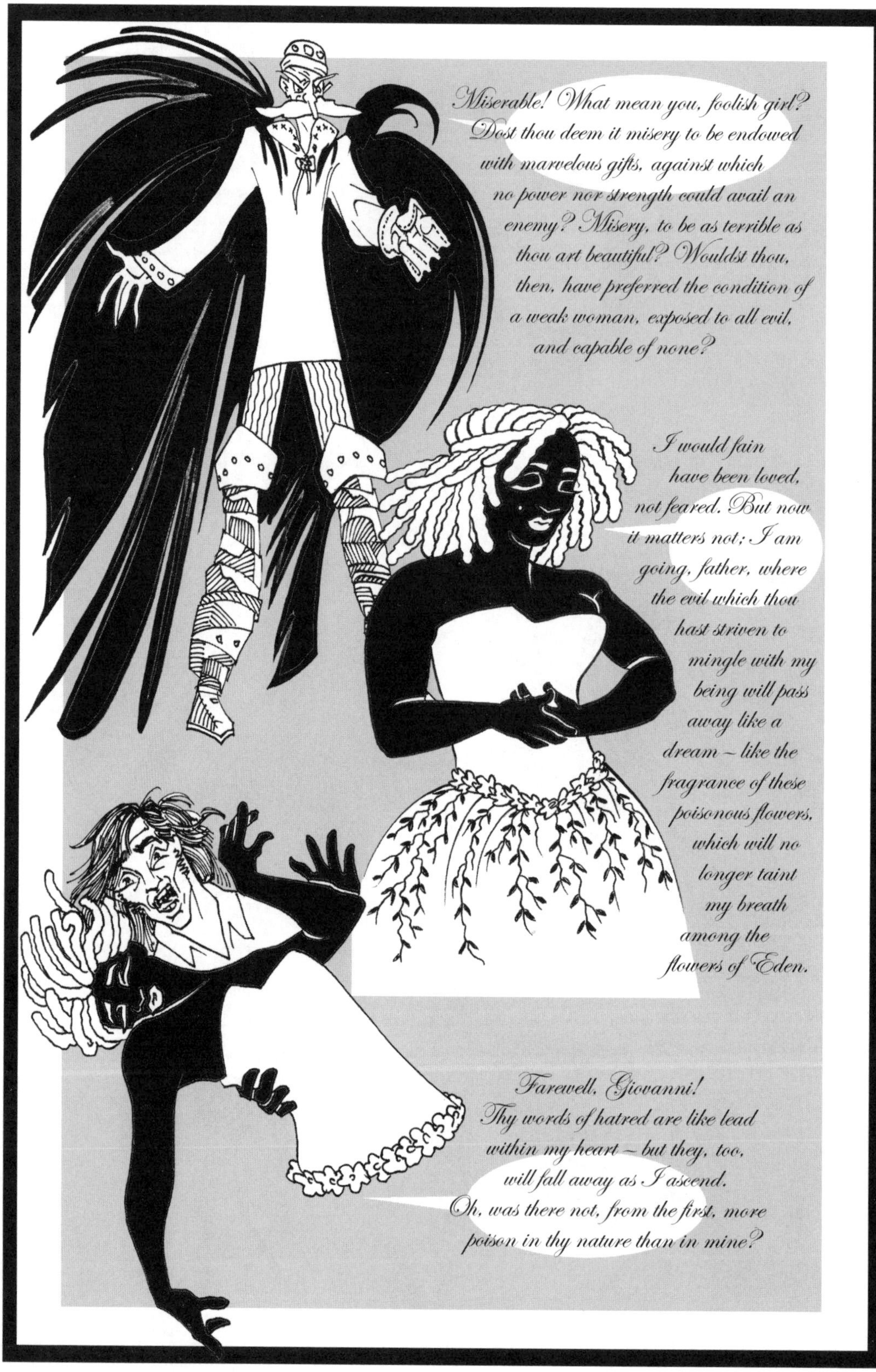
Miserable! What mean you, foolish girl? Dost thou deem it misery to be endowed with marvelous gifts, against which no power nor strength could avail an enemy? Misery, to be as terrible as thou art beautiful? Wouldst thou, then, have preferred the condition of a weak woman, exposed to all evil, and capable of none?
I would fain have been loved, not feared. But now it matters not; I am going, father, where the evil which thou hast striven to mingle with my being will pass away like a dream – like the fragrance of these poisonous flowers, which will no longer taint my breath among the flowers of Eden.
Farewell, Giovanni! Thy words of hatred are like lead within my heart – but they, too, will fall away as I ascend. Oh, was there not, from the first, more poison in thy nature than in mine?

To Beatrice — so radically had her earthly part been wrought upon by Rappaccini's skill — as poison had been life, so the powerful antidote was death. And thus the poor victim of man's ingenuity and of thwarted nature, and of the fatality that attends all such efforts of perverted wisdom, perished there, at the feet of her father and Giovanni. Just at that moment, Professor Pietro Baglioni looked into the garden, and called loudly, in a tone of triumph mixed with horror, to the thunder-stricken man of science:

Rappaccini! Rappaccini! And is this the upshot of your experiment?

ILLUSTRATIONS ©2008 LANCE TOOKS

On the edge of the city lived an accomplished wizard, who passed his time in thoughtful study and studious thought.

This admirable person would have been completely happy but for the numerous interruptions to his studies caused by folk who came to consult him about their troubles.

Knock! Knock! Knock!

Just when he was most deeply interested in his books or engaged in watching the bubbling of a cauldron there would come a knock at his door.

At length these interruptions aroused his anger, and he decided he must have a dog to keep people away from his door.

Hell and damnation!!

THE GLASS DOG

by L. Frank Baum
Adapted by Antonella L. Caputo
Illustrated by Brad Teare

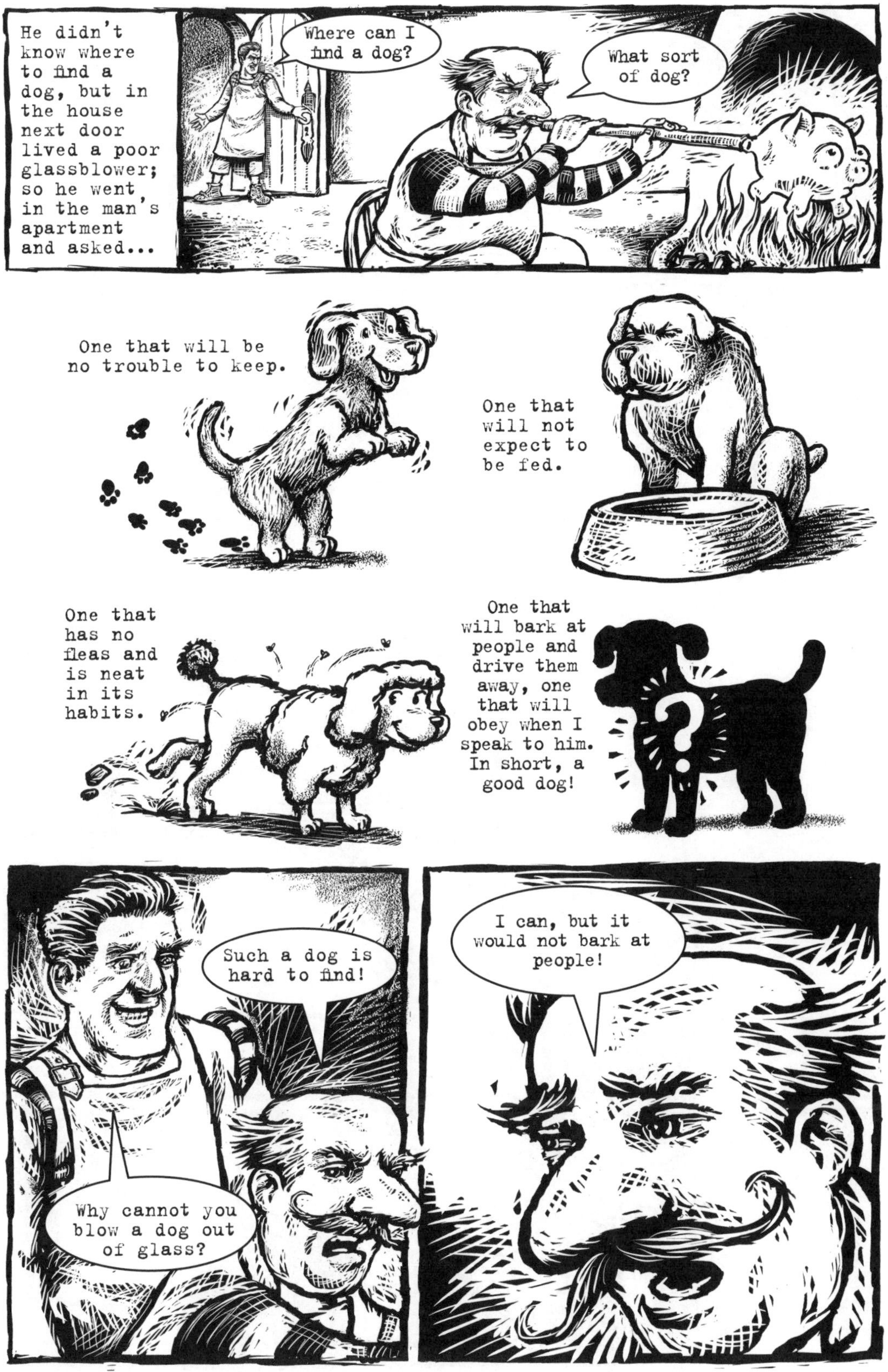
He didn't know where to find a dog, but in the house next door lived a poor glassblower; so he went in the man's apartment and asked...
Where can I find a dog?
What sort of dog?
One that will be no trouble to keep.
One that will not expect to be fed.
One that has no fleas and is neat in its habits.
One that will bark at people and drive them away, one that will obey when I speak to him. In short, a good dog!
Such a dog is hard to find!
Why cannot you blow a dog out of glass?
I can, but it would not bark at people!

Oh, I'll fix that easily enough. If I could not make a glass dog bark I would be a mighty poor wizard!

Very well. I'll be pleased to blow a glass dog for you. Only you must pay for my work.

Certainly, but I have none of that horrid stuff you call money. You must take of my wares in exchange.

Then it's a bargain. I'll start the dog at once.

So the wizard went back to his studies and the glassblower began to make the dog.

Next morning the glassblower entered the wizard's house with the glass dog under his arm.

Could you give me me something to cure my rheumatism?

Oh yes; easily!

What a marvelous dog! What sparkling eyes! You are such a skilled glassblower!

I am glad you like it!

The one drop contained in this vial will cure instantly any kind of disease. It is especially good for rheumatism. But guard it well, for it is the only drop of its kind, and I have forgotten the recipe.

Then the wizard cast a spell and mumbled learned words in the wizardese language over the glass dog, whereupon the little animal first wagged its tail, then began barking in a most frightful manner.

Anecay etrosovay ivivay edway abbaiaway!

WOOF! WOOF!

82

The wizard was delighted at the success of his spell. Immediately he placed the dog outside his door, where it would bark at anyone who dared knock.

My rheumatism is better today. It would be wise to save the medicine for a day when I am very ill.

The glassblower decided not to use the one drop of wizard cure-all and went to work blowing roses out of glass.

The Beautiful Miss Mydas

The Richest Young Lady in Town

The next morning, as the glassblower read his newspaper, he noticed an article stating that Miss Mydas was very ill, and the doctors had given up hope of her recovery.

The glassblower determined to use his precious medicine to better advantage than relieving his own ills.

He walked through the street to the grand mansion where the wealthy Miss Mydas resided.

BAM!

BAM!

No soap, no vegetables, no hair oil, no books! My young lady is dying and we're well supplied for the funeral!

The graveyard won't be needed if you will permit me to speak!

No doctors, sir; they've given up my young lady, and she's given up the doctors!

I am not a doctor. I called to cure your young lady by means of a magical compound!

Step in, please, and take a seat in the hall. I'll speak to the lady's maid.

The lady's maid heard from the glassblower that he had a medicine which would cure her mistress.

But if I restore your mistress to health she must marry me!

I'll make enquiries and see if she's willing!

I'd marry any old thing rather than die! Bring him here at once!

GLUG! GLUG!

The next minute Miss Mydas was as well as she had ever been in her life!

Dear me! I've an engagement at the Fritters' reception tonight! Bring my pearl-colored silk, Maria, and don't forget to cancel the order for the funeral flowers and your mourning gown!

But Miss Mydas! You promised to marry me if I cured you!

I know, but we must have time to make the proper announcements to to the society papers and have the wedding cards engraved. Call me tomorrow and we'll talk it over.

The man went home filled with joy; he was about to marry a rich wife who would keep him in luxury forever afterward.

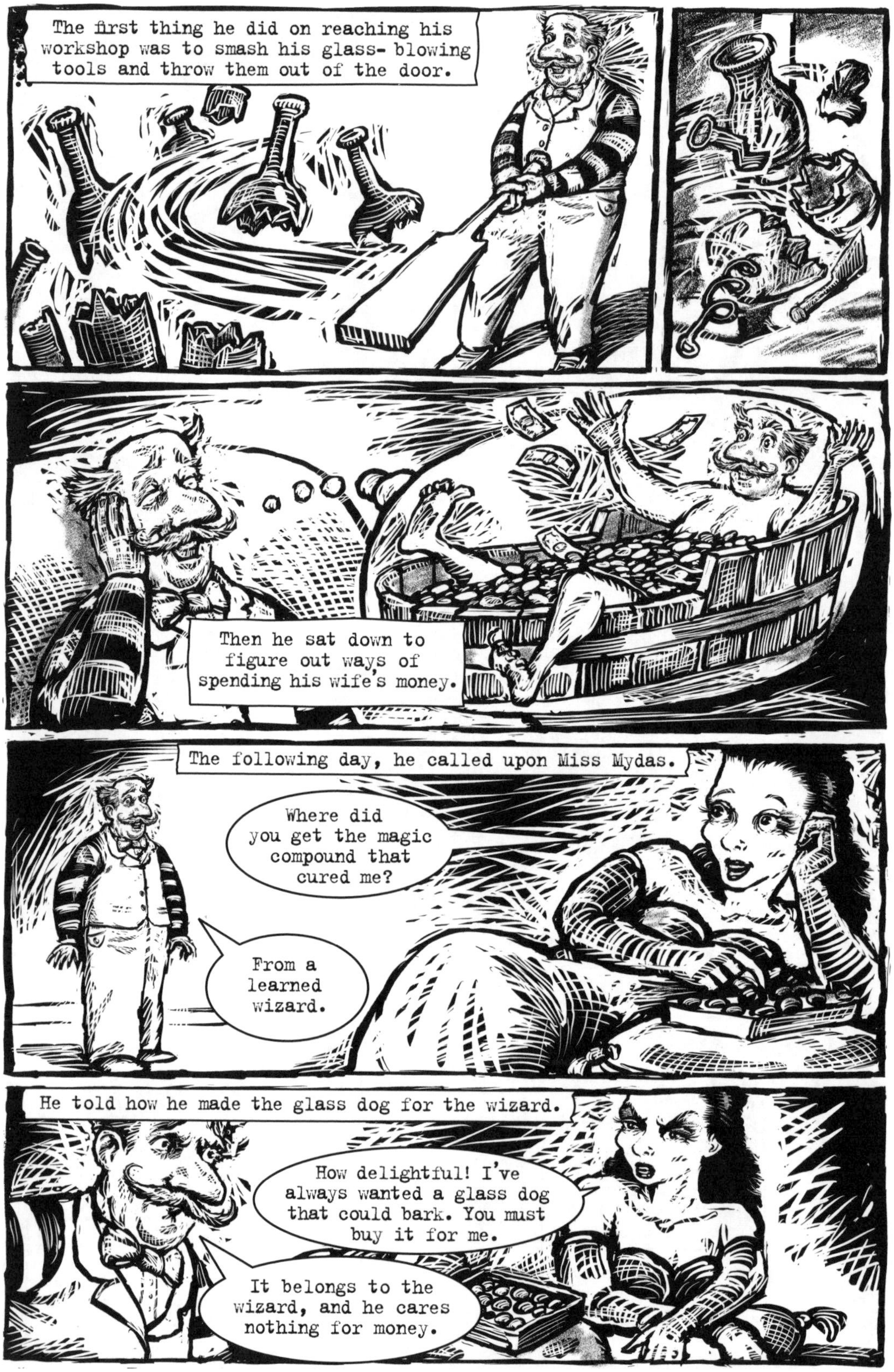
The first thing he did on reaching his workshop was to smash his glass- blowing tools and throw them out of the door.
Then he sat down to figure out ways of spending his wife's money.
The following day, he called upon Miss Mydas.
Where did you get the magic compound that cured me?
From a learned wizard.
He told how he made the glass dog for the wizard.
How delightful! I've always wanted a glass dog that could bark. You must buy it for me.
It belongs to the wizard, and he cares nothing for money.

Then you must steal it for me! I can never live happily unless I have a glass dog that can bark!

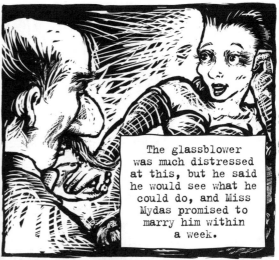

The glassblower was much distressed at this, but he said he would see what he could do, and Miss Mydas promised to marry him within a week.

On his way home he purchased a heavy sack.

The next day he sent the sack by a messenger boy to Miss Mydas.

In the afternoon he called upon her in person, feeling quite sure he would be received with gratitude.

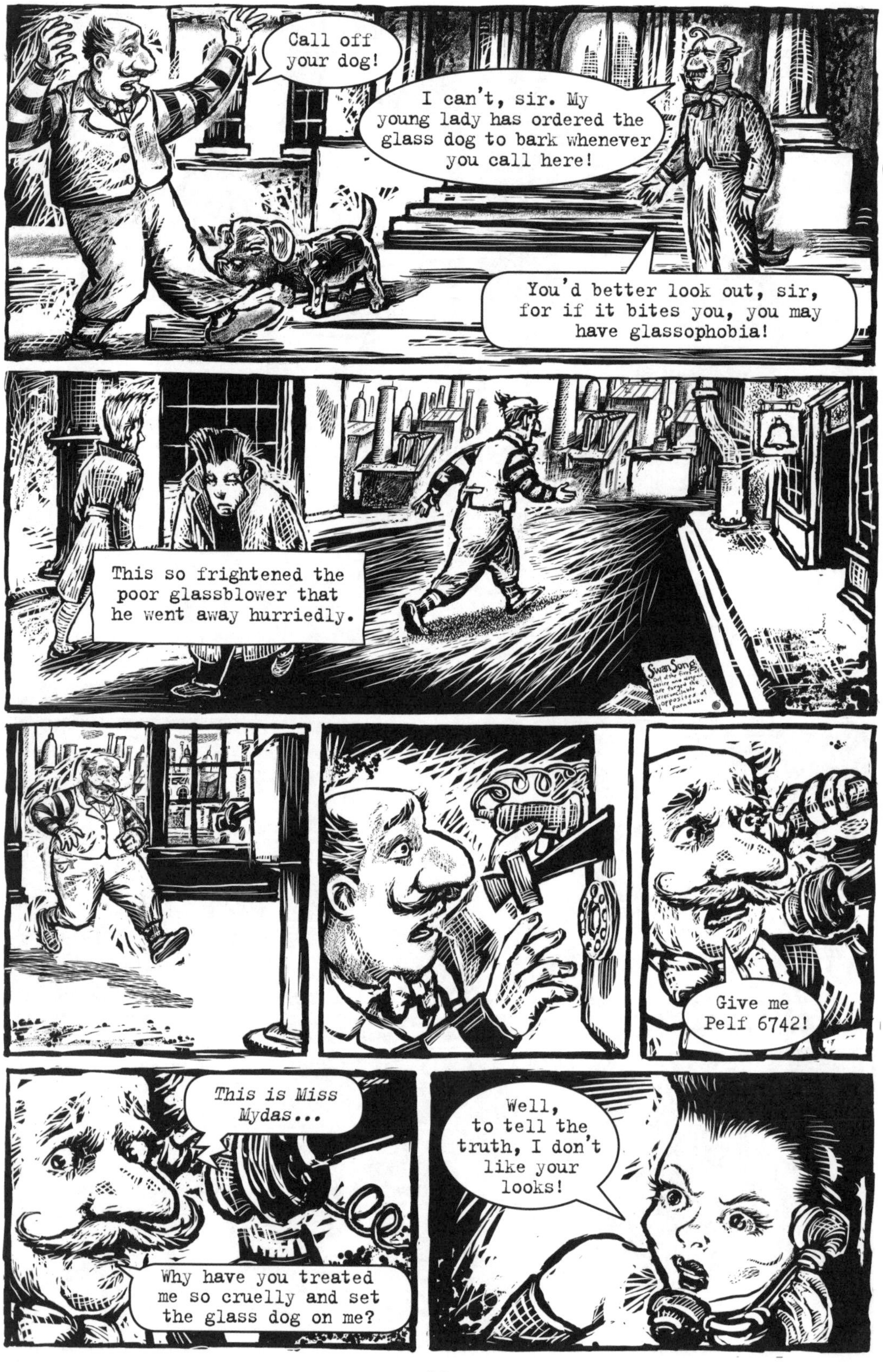
Call off your dog!
I can't, sir. My young lady has ordered the glass dog to bark whenever you call here!
You'd better look out, sir, for if it bites you, you may have glassophobia!
This so frightened the poor glassblower that he went away hurriedly.
Swan Song
Give me Pelf 6742!
This is Miss Mydas...
Why have you treated me so cruelly and set the glass dog on me?
Well, to tell the truth, I don't like your looks!

Your cheeks are pale and baggy, your hair is coarse and long, your eyes are small and red, your hands are big and rough and you are bow-legged!

But I can't help my looks! And you promised to marry me!

If you were better-looking I'd keep my promise. But unless you keep away from my mansion I shall set my glass dog on you!

The miserable glass-blower went home with a heart bursting with disappointment.

Knock! Knock!

He began tying a rope to the bedpost by which to hang himself when someone knocked at the door.

I've lost my dog! Someone has stolen him!

Have you indeed? That's too bad.

89

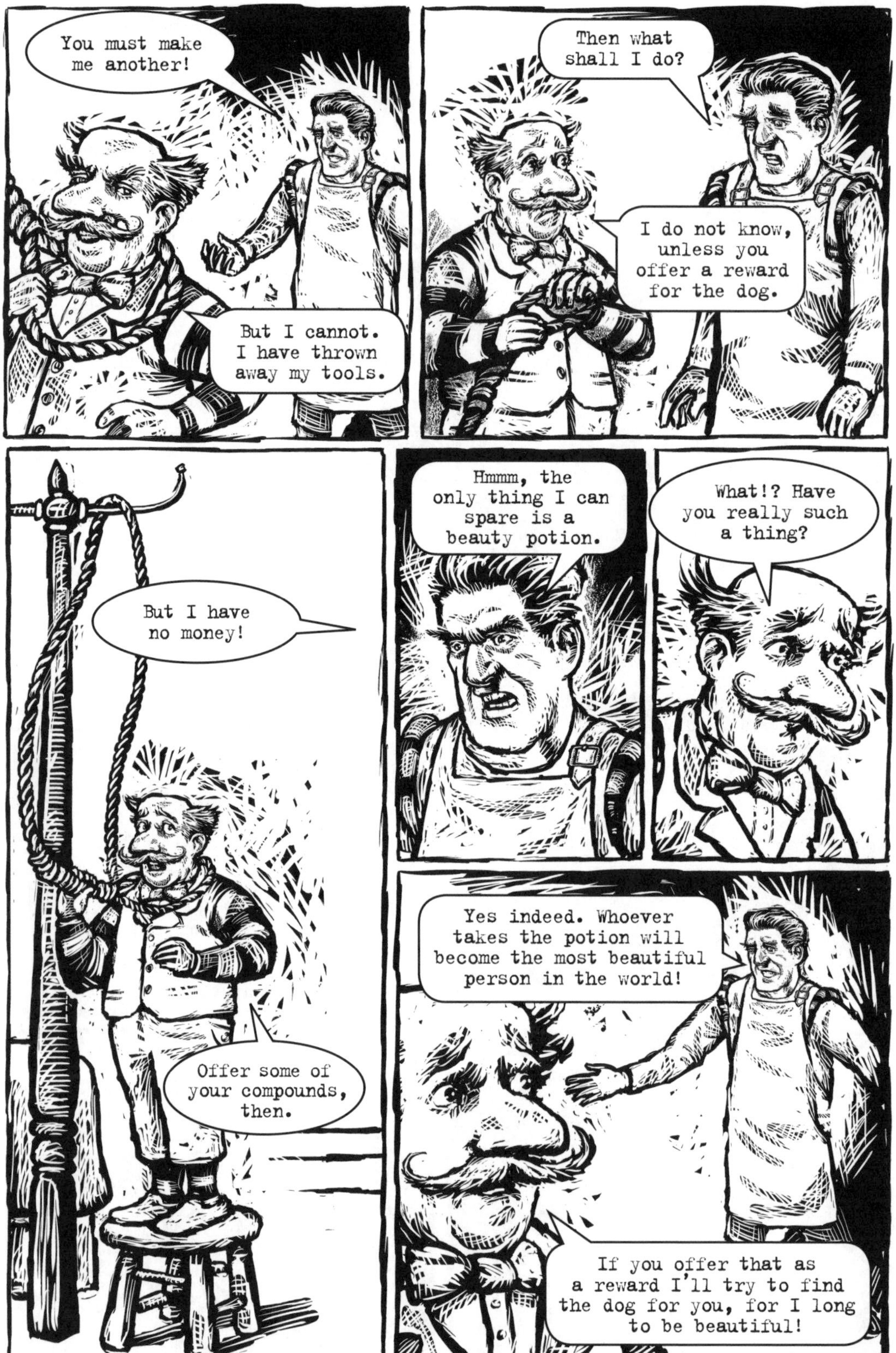
You must make me another!
But I cannot. I have thrown away my tools.
Then what shall I do?
I do not know, unless you offer a reward for the dog.
But I have no money!
Offer some of your compounds, then.
Hmmm, the only thing I can spare is a beauty potion.
What!? Have you really such a thing?
Yes indeed. Whoever takes the potion will become the most beautiful person in the world!
If you offer that as a reward I'll try to find the dog for you, for I long to be beautiful!

So the glassblower went out and pretended to look, and by-and-by he returned to the wizard.

I've discovered the dog. You will find him in the mansion of Miss Mydas.

The wizard went at once to see if this was true, and, sure enough, the glass dog ran out and began barking at him.

The wizard spread his hands and chanted a magic spell which sent the dog fast asleep.

Anecay etrosovay ORMIDAY!

Then he picked him up and carried him to his house.

Humph!

Afterward he brought the beauty potion to the glassblower as a reward.

The fellow immediately swallowed it...

...and...

POOF!

...became the most beautiful man in the world!

ZAP!

He called upon Miss Mydas and when the young lady saw him she fell in love with his beauty at once.

If only you were a count or a prince I'd willingly marry you!

But I AM a prince! The PRINCE of glassblowers!

Ah! Then if you are willing to accept an allowance of four dollars a week I'll order the wedding cards engraved.

The man hesitated, but when he thought of the alternative he consented to the terms.

And so they were married.

FLASH!

But the bride was very jealous of her husband's beauty and led him a dog's life.

So he managed to get into debt...

...and made her miserable in turn.

As for the glass dog, the wizard set him barking again. I suppose he is there yet...

I am rather sorry, for I should like to consult the wizard about the moral of this story.

THE END!

94

The Dream-Bridge
by Clark Ashton Smith / illustrated by Evert Geradts

All drear and barren seemed the hours,
    That passed rain-swept and tempest-blown.
The dead leaves fell like brownish notes
    Within the rain's grey monotone.

There came a lapse between the showers:
    The clouds grew rich with sunset gleams;
Then o'er the sky a rainbow sprang —
    A bridge unto the Land of Dreams.

95

Three times I dreamed of the marvelous city, and three times it was snatched away from me.

All golden and lovely it blazed in the sunset, a fever of the gods. Mystery hung about it as clouds about a fabulous unvisited mountain.

And as I stood breathless and expectant there swept up in me the poignancy and suspense of almost vanished memory, the pain of lost things. Vaguely it called up glimpses of a far forgotten youth, when wonder and pleasure lay in all the mystery of days.

But each night as I looked off over that hushed sunset city of beauty and unearthly immanence I felt the bondage of dream's tyrannous gods!

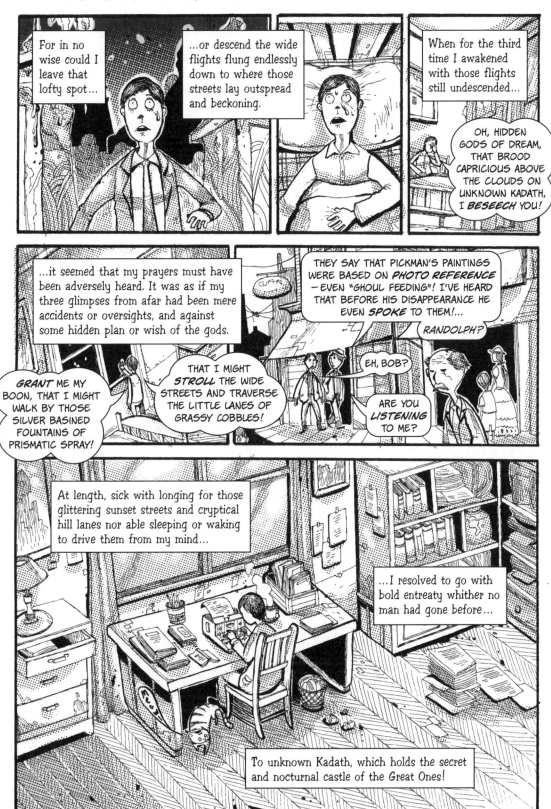

For in no wise could I leave that lofty spot...

...or descend the wide flights flung endlessly down to where those streets lay outspread and beckoning.

When for the third time I awakened with those flights still undescended...

OH, HIDDEN GODS OF DREAM, THAT BROOD CAPRICIOUS ABOVE THE CLOUDS ON UNKNOWN KADATH, I *BESEECH* YOU!

...it seemed that my prayers must have been adversely heard. It was as if my three glimpses from afar had been mere accidents or oversights, and against some hidden plan or wish of the gods.

THEY SAY THAT PICKMAN'S PAINTINGS WERE BASED ON *PHOTO REFERENCE* —EVEN "GHOUL FEEDING"! I'VE HEARD THAT BEFORE HIS DISAPPEARANCE HE EVEN *SPOKE* TO THEM!...

RANDOLPH?

EH, BOB?

ARE YOU *LISTENING* TO ME?

GRANT ME MY BOON, THAT I MIGHT WALK BY THOSE SILVER BASINED FOUNTAINS OF PRISMATIC SPRAY!

THAT I MIGHT *STROLL* THE WIDE STREETS AND TRAVERSE THE LITTLE LANES OF GRASSY COBBLES!

At length, sick with longing for those glittering sunset streets and cryptical hill lanes nor able sleeping or waking to drive them from my mind...

...I resolved to go with bold entreaty whither no man had gone before...

To unknown Kadath, which holds the secret and nocturnal castle of the Great Ones!

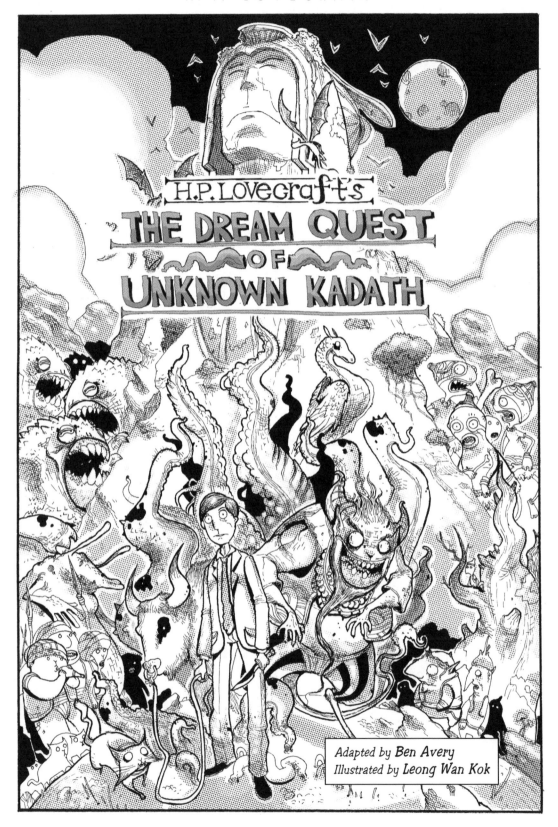

H.P. Lovecraft's
THE DREAM QUEST
OF
UNKNOWN KADATH

Adapted by *Ben Avery*
Illustrated by *Leong Wan Kok*

And so, in light slumber...

...I descended the seventy steps to the cavern of flame, where I spoke of my design to the priests Nasht and Kaman-Thah.

GREETINGS, WISE ONES. I SEEK YOUR AID, AS I WISH TO TRAVEL TO UNKNOWN KADATH, WHERE I MAY ASK OF THE GREAT ONES A BOON.

I HAVE PRAYED AND MADE MY DESIRES KNOWN TO THEM, YET THEY IGNORE MY PETITION!

RANDOLPH CARTER, THAT IS MOST UNWISE!

IT WOULD MEAN THE DEATH OF YOUR SOUL!

IN THEIR SILENCE, THE GREAT ONES HAVE MADE THEIR WISHES KNOWN!

IT IS NOT AGREEABLE TO THEM TO BE HARASSED BY INCESSANT PLEAS.

ALSO, NOT ONLY HAS NO MAN EVER BEEN TO *KADATH*, NONE EVEN KNOW WHERE IT MIGHT BE!

BUT IF IT LIES IN *ANOTHER* DREAMLAND... ONLY THREE HAVE EVER CROSSED AND RECROSSED THE BLACK IMPIOUS GULFS TO OTHER DREAMLANDS, AND TWO CAME BACK *QUITE MAD.*

BUT I *MUST* FIND IT! ONLY *THEY* CAN GRANT ME ACCESS TO WHAT I DESIRE — FOR *THEY* HAVE *TAKEN* IT FROM ME!

IF *KADATH* BE IN *OUR* DREAMLAND, IT MIGHT CONCEIVABLY BE REACHED —

...WHO GNAWS HUNGRILY AMIDST THE BEAT OF VILE DRUMS AND THE MONOTONOUS WHINE OF ACCURSED FLUTES...

FOR OUTSIDE THE ORDERED UNIVERSE — AT THE CENTER OF ALL INFINITY — LIES THE BOUNDLESS DAEMON *AZATHOTH...*

...TO WHICH DETESTABLE POUNDING AND PIPING DANCE THE MINDLESS *OTHER GODS* WHOSE SOUL AND MESSENGER IS THE CRAWLING CHAOS *NYARLATHOTEP!*

FRIENDS, I THANK YOU FOR YOUR CONCERN. BUT I AM AN EXPERIENCED DREAMER, WITH MANY MEMORIES AND DEVICES TO AID ME ON THIS PATH.

So, asking a formal blessing of the priests and thinking shrewdly on my course, I boldly descended the seven hundred steps to the Gate of Deeper Slumber...

...and set out through the enchanted wood.

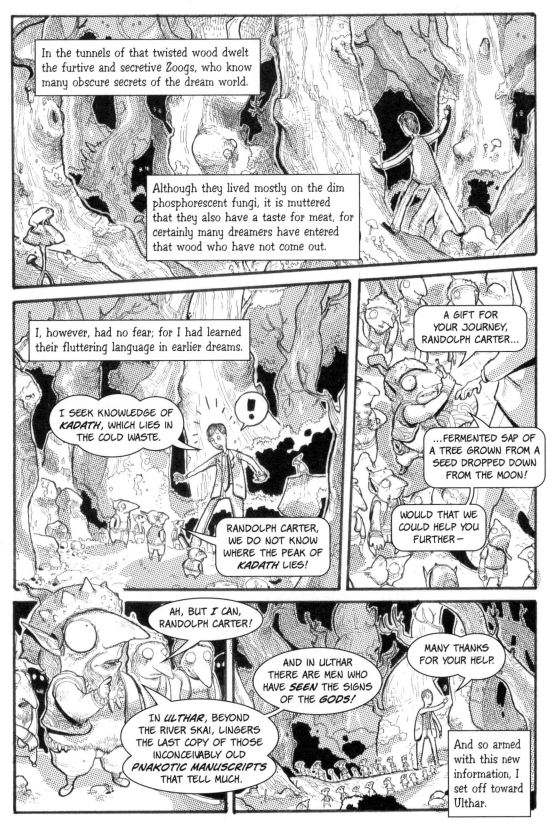

In the tunnels of that twisted wood dwelt the furtive and secretive Zoogs, who know many obscure secrets of the dream world.

Although they lived mostly on the dim phosphorescent fungi, it is muttered that they also have a taste for meat, for certainly many dreamers have entered that wood who have not come out.

I, however, had no fear; for I had learned their fluttering language in earlier dreams.

I SEEK KNOWLEDGE OF *KADATH*, WHICH LIES IN THE COLD WASTE.

!

RANDOLPH CARTER, WE DO NOT KNOW WHERE THE PEAK OF *KADATH* LIES!

A GIFT FOR YOUR JOURNEY, RANDOLPH CARTER...

...FERMENTED SAP OF A TREE GROWN FROM A SEED DROPPED DOWN FROM THE MOON!

WOULD THAT WE COULD HELP YOU FURTHER—

AH, BUT *I* CAN, RANDOLPH CARTER!

IN *ULTHAR*, BEYOND THE RIVER SKAI, LINGERS THE LAST COPY OF THOSE INCONCEIVABLY OLD *PNAKOTIC MANUSCRIPTS* THAT TELL MUCH.

AND IN ULTHAR THERE ARE MEN WHO HAVE *SEEN* THE SIGNS OF THE *GODS!*

MANY THANKS FOR YOUR HELP.

And so armed with this new information, I set off toward Ulthar.

101

Behind me crept several of the curious Zoogs, for they wished to learn what might befall me, and bear my legend back to their people.

When I came to the edge of the wood, the strengthening glow told me it was the twilight of morning.

After the enchanted wood were fertile plains, hedges and plowed fields, and the thatched roofs of a peaceful land.

Soon, the frequent presence of cats revealed Ulthar, for in Ulthar, according to an ancient and significant law, no man may kill a cat...

...though the cats were somewhat dispersed by the presence of the Zoogs!

I made my way directly to the modest Temple of the Elder Ones where the priests and old records were said to be.

Within the temple, I sought out the patriarch Atal.

IT IS *LUCKY* THAT NO MAN KNOWS WHERE THE ONYX STRONGHOLD ATOP *KADATH* TOWERS, FOR THE FRUITS OF ASCENDING IT WOULD BE *VERY GRAVE.*

WHAT CAN YOU TELL ME ABOUT THE MARVELOUS *SUNSET CITY?*

HRMMM...

EARTH'S LESSER GODS ARE PROTECTED BY THE *OTHER GODS* FROM OUTSIDE, WHOM IT IS BETTER *NOT* TO DISCUSS.

IT IS MUCH BETTER TO LEAVE THEM ALONE EXCEPT IN TACTFUL PRAYERS.

PROBABLY THAT PLACE BELONGS TO YOUR *OWN* DREAM WORLD, AND NOT TO THE GENERAL LAND OF VISION THAT MANY KNOW. BUT THE STOPPING OF THE DREAM SHOWS CLEARLY THAT IT IS SOMETHING THE *GREAT ONES* WISH TO HIDE FROM YOU

I CAN BE OF NO HELP TO YOU.

Then, I did a wicked thing—

A GIFT... FOR MY GRACIOUS HOST.

AH, THANK YOU, SON.

I offered my guileless host so many draughts of the moonwine that the old man became irresponsibly talkative.

...THEY SAY THAT CARVED ON THE SOLID ROCK OF THE MOUNTAIN *NGRANEK* IS A LIKENESS WHICH EARTH'S GODS ONCE WROUGHT OF THEIR OWN FEATURES... MY! THIS IS GOOD ALE!

TAKE ANOTHER DRINK, ATAL. I HAVE HAD MY FILL.

...OF COURSE, I KNOW NOT WHERE TO FIND *NGRANEK* EITHER...*HIC!*... PERHAPS BETTER TRAVELED TRADERS FROM THE PORTS WOULD KNOW...

Outside, I heard a faint caterwauling and spitting.

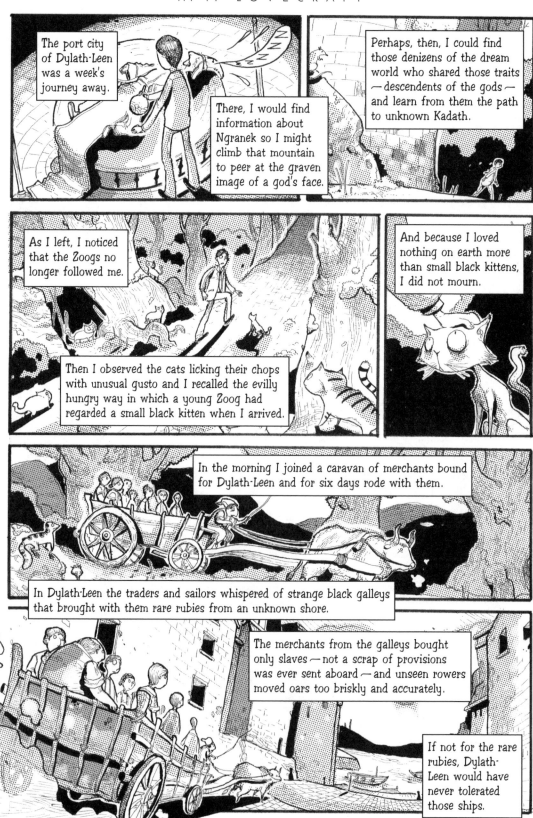

The port city of Dylath-Leen was a week's journey away.

There, I would find information about Ngranek so I might climb that mountain to peer at the graven image of a god's face.

Perhaps, then, I could find those denizens of the dream world who shared those traits —descendents of the gods— and learn from them the path to unknown Kadath.

As I left, I noticed that the Zoogs no longer followed me.

And because I loved nothing on earth more than small black kittens, I did not mourn.

Then I observed the cats licking their chops with unusual gusto and I recalled the evilly hungry way in which a young Zoog had regarded a small black kitten when I arrived.

In the morning I joined a caravan of merchants bound for Dylath-Leen and for six days rode with them.

In Dylath-Leen the traders and sailors whispered of strange black galleys that brought with them rare rubies from an unknown shore.

The merchants from the galleys bought only slaves —not a scrap of provisions was ever sent aboard— and unseen rowers moved oars too briskly and accurately.

If not for the rare rubies, Dylath-Leen would have never tolerated those ships.

But I found no tales of Kadath or the carved image on Ngranek.

...AND YOU KNOW WHAT'S *UNNATURAL* LIKE?—THEM *BLACK GALLEYS*, COME INTO PORT F'R WEEKS WHILE THEIR MERCHANTS TRADE, BUT NARY A SIGN OF THE CREW!

YES, BUT DO YOU KNOW ANYTHING OF *KADATH* IN THE COLD WASTE?

NE'ER 'EARD OF IT!

BUT SEE *'IM* THERE? THEY SAYS 'E TRADES WITH THE 'ORRIBLE STONE VILLAGES ON THE ICY DESERT PLATEAU OF *LENG*...

When a black galley slipped into the harbor, silent and alien, and with a strange stench that the south wind drove into the town, uneasiness rustled through the taverns along that waterfront.

'E'S EVEN RUMORED TO 'AVE DEALT WITH THAT *HIGH PRIEST* NOT TO BE DESCRIBED—Y'KNOW, THE ONE WHAT WEARS A YELLOW SILKEN *MASK* OVER ITS FACE. *'E'LL* 'AVE YER ANSWERS!

I observed the merchants closely, and disliked them more the longer I looked at them.

Then I saw them drive the stout men of Parg up the gangplank grunting and sweating, and wondered what fate those pathetic creatures might be destined to serve.

On the third evening of that galley's stay, the dark merchant I had seen earlier spoke to me, smirking sinfully and hinting of what he'd heard of my quest.

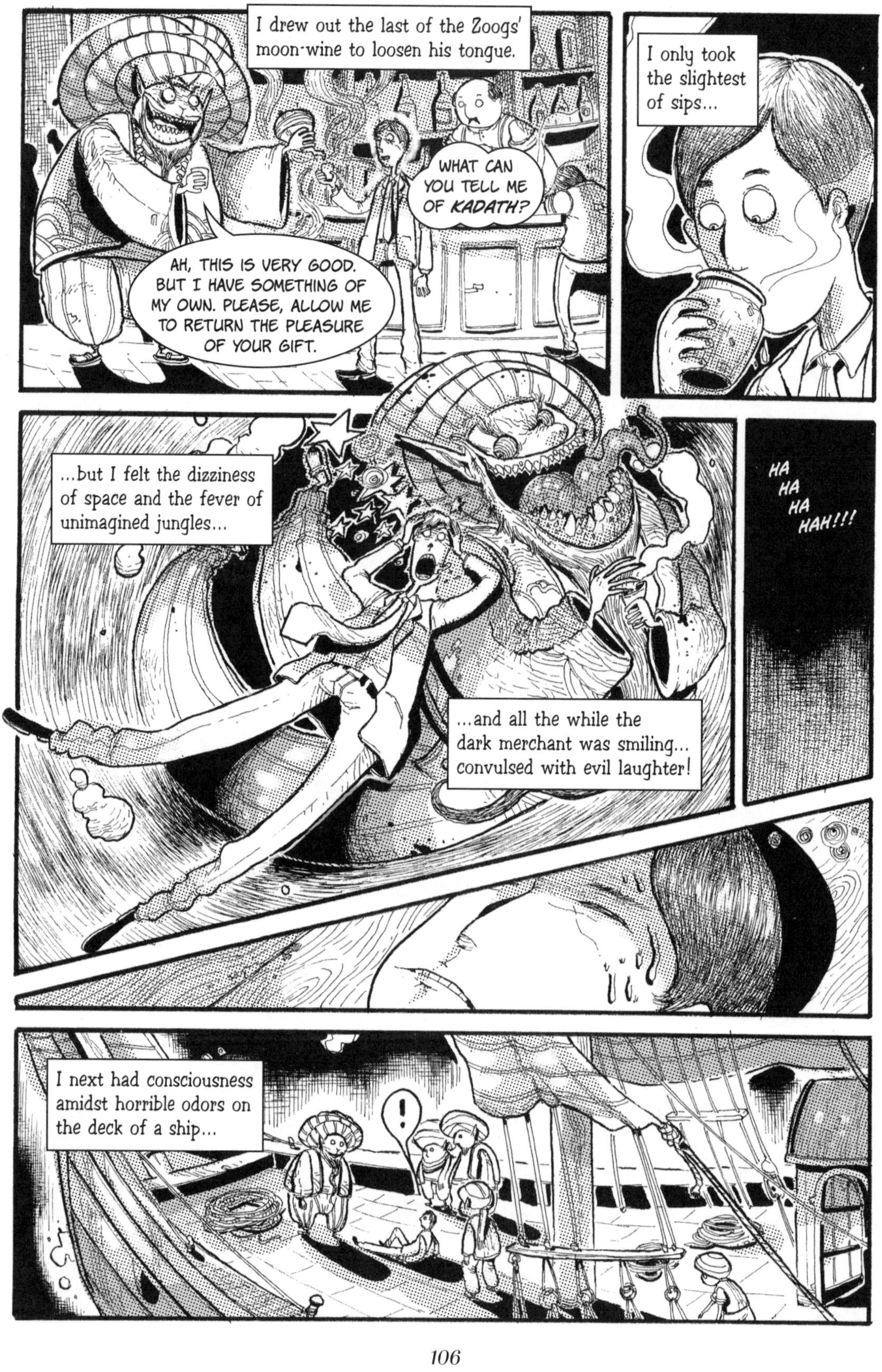
I drew out the last of the Zoogs' moon-wine to loosen his tongue.
WHAT CAN YOU TELL ME OF *KADATH?*
AH, THIS IS VERY GOOD. BUT I HAVE SOMETHING OF MY OWN. PLEASE, ALLOW ME TO RETURN THE PLEASURE OF YOUR GIFT.
I only took the slightest of sips...
...but I felt the dizziness of space and the fever of unimagined jungles...
...and all the while the dark merchant was smiling... convulsed with evil laughter!
HA HA HA HAH!!!
I next had consciousness amidst horrible odors on the deck of a ship...
!

...flying toward the moon!

The sardonic merchants gave no word of their intent, though I well knew they must be leagued with those who wished to hold me from my quest.

For in the land of dream the Other Gods have many agents moving among men...

...eager to work for the favor of their hideous soul and messenger...

...the Crawling Chaos, Nyarlathotep!

WHERE ARE YOU TAKING ME?

The whining of hellish piping was my only answer: the toad things had no voices, and the slaves did not talk.

I could not doubt that at our destination the Crawling Chaos waited.

The impious flutes were maddening, and I would have given worlds for some even half-normal sound—

Then, through that star specked darkness there did come a familiar call!

RRRRWOOUU!!!!

It was the midnight yell of the cat—

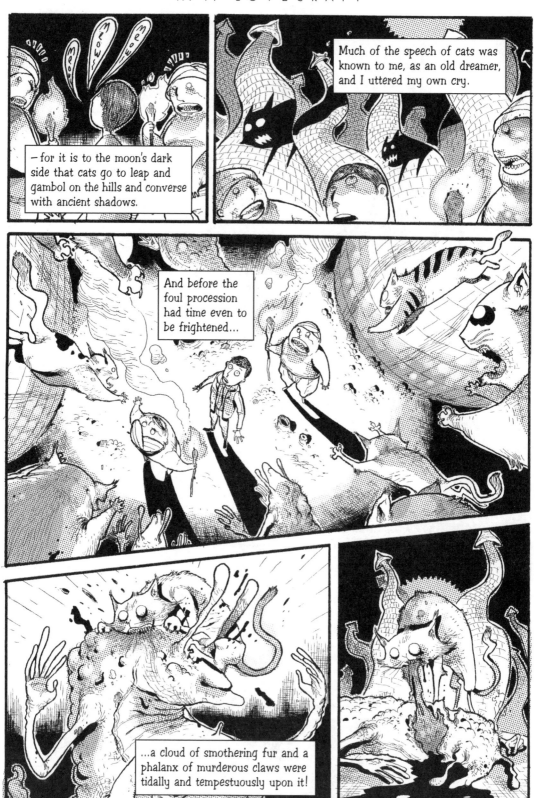

—for it is to the moon's dark side that cats go to leap and gambol on the hills and converse with ancient shadows.

Much of the speech of cats was known to me, as an old dreamer, and I uttered my own cry.

And before the foul procession had time even to be frightened...

...a cloud of smothering fur and a phalanx of murderous claws were tidally and tempestuously upon it!

It was a stupendous sight...

The flutes stopped, and there were shrieks in the night.

I had never before seen so many cats. Black, grey, and white; yellow, tiger, and mixed; Persian, Angora, and Egyptian; all were there in the fury of battle!

Dying almost-humans screamed, and cats spit and yowled and roared!

But the toad-things made never a sound as their stinking green ichor oozed fatally.

At last awe and exhaustion closed my eyes, and when I opened them again it was upon a strange scene.

Morning brought with it the great shining disk of the earth.

MANY THANKS, MY FRIENDS.

I was freed of the obscene fate that awaited me at the end of that foul procession, but I found myself stranded.

YOUR FRIENDSHIP WITH OUR SPECIES IS WELL KNOWN, RANDOLPH CARTER.

MY TROOPS WILL TAKE YOU ANYWHERE YOU DESIRE.

TO DYLATH-LEEN THEN, FOR I WISH TO WARN THEM TO HAVE NO MORE TRAFFIC WITH THE BLACK GALLEYS.

THEN LET YOURSELF BE BORNE ALONG SMOOTHLY AND PASSIVELY...

AND NOW... LEAP! LEAP!!!

The leap of the cats was very swift, and behind me I left the Crawling Chaos Nyarlathotep vainly waiting for me.

Returning to Dylath-Leen, I said what I could against the black galleys and their infamous ways.

Yet so fond were the jewelers of those great rubies that none would promise to cease trafficking.

I sailed out of Dylath-Leen on a barque of wholesome men carrying a cargo of fragrant resin, delicate pottery, and strange figures carved of Ngranek's lava.

I DOUBT ANY LIVING HAVE SEEN THE CARVING ON MOUNT NGRANEK, FOR THE CLIMB IS BARREN AND SINISTER...

AND THERE ARE RUMORS OF A CAVE WHEREIN DWELL THE *NIGHT-GAUNTS!*

ASK THE LAVA GATHERERS AND IMAGE MAKERS, THEY MIGHT HELP YOU IN YOUR QUEST.

I took quarter in an ancient tavern, where I laid my plans for the ascent of Ngranek.

The keeper of the tavern was a very old man, and had heard many legends.

NONE LIVING HAVE SEEN WHAT YOU SEEK—BUT COME WITH ME.

MY GREAT-GRANDFATHER HEARD FROM *HIS* GREAT GRANDFATHER THAT THERE WAS A MAN WHO HAD CLIMBED *NGRANEK* AND SEEN THE CARVEN FACE.

THAT WAS IN THE DAYS WHEN MEN WERE BOLDER AND LESS RELUCTANT TO VISIT THE HIGHER SLOPES.

HE SCRATCHED IT HERE IN THE CLAY WALL FOR OTHERS TO BEHOLD...

The rendering of the face on the wall was hasty and careless, and wholly over-shadowed by a crowd of little companion shapes in the worst possible taste, with horns and wings and claws and curling tails.

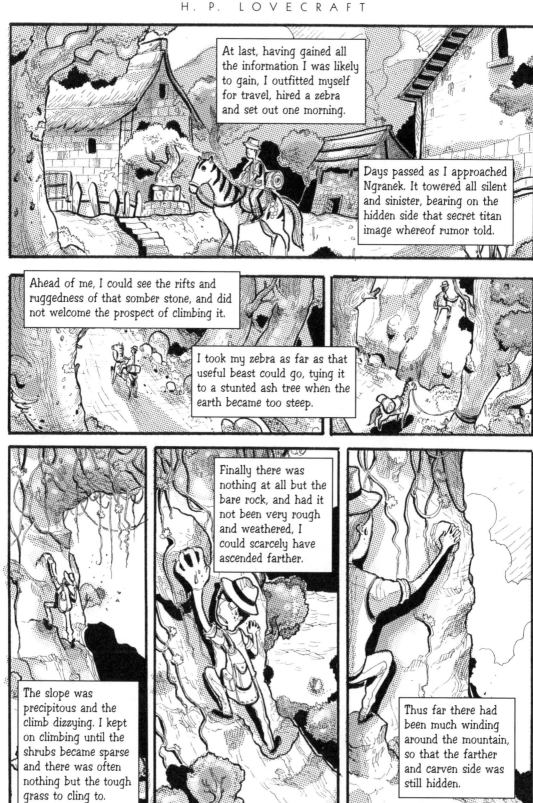

At last, having gained all the information I was likely to gain, I outfitted myself for travel, hired a zebra and set out one morning.

Days passed as I approached Ngranek. It towered all silent and sinister, bearing on the hidden side that secret titan image whereof rumor told.

Ahead of me, I could see the rifts and ruggedness of that somber stone, and did not welcome the prospect of climbing it.

I took my zebra as far as that useful beast could go, tying it to a stunted ash tree when the earth became too steep.

Finally there was nothing at all but the bare rock, and had it not been very rough and weathered, I could scarcely have ascended farther.

The slope was precipitous and the climb dizzying. I kept on climbing until the shrubs became sparse and there was often nothing but the tough grass to cling to.

Thus far there had been much winding around the mountain, so that the farther and carven side was still hidden.

I now saw a ledge running upward and to the left which seemed to head the way I wished.

I considered the tales of night-gaunts as I noticed the many small caves set in the mountain wall.

But all lesser thoughts were lost in the wish to see that carven face which might set me on the track of the gods atop unknown Kadath.

Poised in windy insecurity miles above earth, with only space and death on one side and only slippery walls of rock on the other I was for a moment shaken with doubt lest it prove impassable.

But there was a way. Only a very expert dreamer could have used those imperceptible footholds, yet to me they were sufficient.

I felt from the chill that I must be near the snow line, and when I saw a crag I gasped aloud, and clutched at the jagged rock in awe...

It gleamed red and stupendous in the sunset with the carved and polished features of a god.

Stern and terrible shone that face that the sunset lit with fire.

It was a god chiseled by the hands of the gods, and it looked down haughty and majestic upon the seeker.

Here, too, was the added marvel of recognition; for the image was the kin of such as I had seen often in the taverns of the seaport Celephaïs which lies in Ooth-Nargai! It was clear that these could be no others than the demi-gods I sought.

Where they dwelt, there must the cold waste lie close, and within it unknown Kadath and its onyx castle for the Great Ones!

So to Celephaïs I must go, returning back the way I came back to Dylath-Leen and again into the enchanted wood of the Zoogs, to the gilded spires of Thran, where I might find a galleon bound over the Cerenarian Sea.

Perched on that ledge night found me; and in the blackness I might neither go down nor go up, but only cling and shiver in that narrow place 'til the day came, praying to keep awake lest sleep loose my hold.

Suddenly, I felt a rush of air above me in the dark.

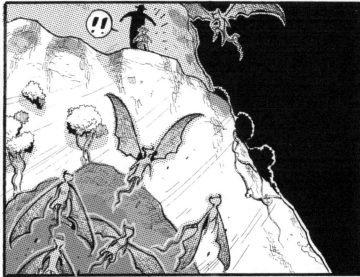

Night-gaunts. They made no sound at all themselves, and even their membranous wings were silent. They were frightfully cold and damp and slippery, and their paws kneaded one detestably.

Soon we were plunging hideously downward through inconceivable abysses in a whirling, sickening rush of dank, tomb-like air.

Then they left me alone in that black valley. To bring me thither was the duty of the night-gaunts that guard Ngranek; and this done, they flapped away silently.

I knew that I was in the dreaded vale of Pnoth, where the ghouls of the waking world cast the refuse of their feastings...

...and where crawl and burrow the enormous Dholes, terrible creatures known only by dim rumor.

I did not wish to meet a Dhole.

A man I had known in Boston — a painter of strange pictures — had actually made friends with the ghouls and had taught me the simpler part of their disgusting meeping and glibbering.

I sent up as best as I might that meeping cry which is the call of the ghoul.

An answering glibber told me that a rope ladder would be lowered.

But my shouting had also been heard by something else, and I heard a vague rustling in the bones a way off.

As this ominously approached, I became more and more uncomfortable; for I did not wish to move away from the spot where the ladder would come.

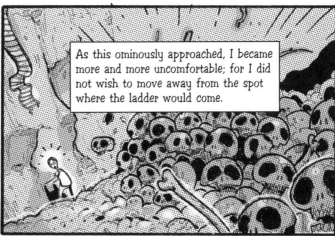

The sound did not cease, and followed me even as I climbed.

At a height which must have been fifteen or twenty feet I felt my whole side brushed by a great slippery length which grew alternately convex and concave with wriggling!

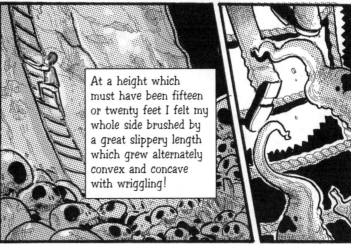

I climbed with aching and blistered hands, desperate to leave behind me that loathsome and overfed Dhole....

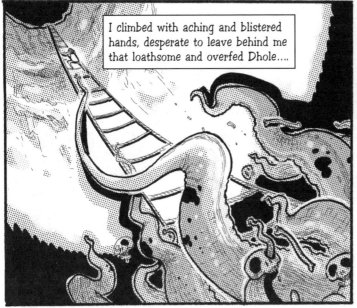

...at last discerning above me the projecting edge of the great crag of the ghouls!

Then I saw a curious face peering over it as a gargoyle peers over a parapet of Notre Dame. This almost made me lose my hold through faintness.

A moment later I was myself again; for my friend Richard Pickman had once introduced me to a ghoul, and I knew well their slumping forms and unmentionable idiosyncrasies.

The ghouls were in general respectful, even if one did attempt to pinch me while several others eyed my leanness speculatively.

Through patient glibbering I made inquiries regarding my vanished friend, and found he had become a ghoul of some prominence in abysses nearer the waking world.

HEL. LO. CAR. TER.

PICKMAN! GREAT GODS, IT *IS* YOU!

WHY. COME. YOU. HERE.

I WISH TO GET TO THE CITY *CELEPHAIS* IN *OOTH-NARGAI*, VIA THE ENCHANTED WOOD OF THE *ZOOGS*.

YOU. FIND. DOOM. YOU. FIND. DEATH. YOU. FIND... *GUGS*.

BUT I *MUST* GO, IF I AM TO FIND THE ANSWERS THAT I SEEK!

DOOR. OF. STONE. CONN. ECTS. GHOUL. LAND. WITH. ZOOG. LAND.

DOOR. IN. GUG. LAND.

I *MUST* GET THERE, SO I CAN JOURNEY ON TO UNKNOWN *KADATH*, WHERE I CAN FIND THE *SUNSET CITY*— THE OBJECT OF MY OBSESSION.

The Gugs — hairy and gigantic mortal dreamer eaters!

OBB. SESS. SHUN.

VER. EEE. WELL.

Finally Pickman consented to guide me inside the great wall of the *Gugs'* kingdom and through that twilight realm of circular stone towers to the great stone door.

Pickman even consented to lend three ghouls to help with a tombstone lever in raising the door.

I followed the loping three through the dark streets of rough pavement, hearing with disgust the abominable muffled snortings from great black doorways which marked the slumber of the Gugs.

At last, we began a climb of interminable length in utter blackness.

All through the endless climb there lurked peril...

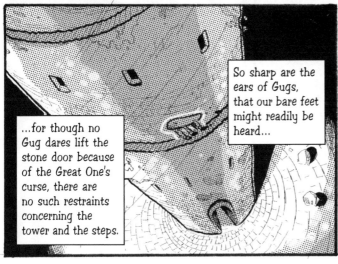

...for though no Gug dares lift the stone door because of the *Great One's* curse, there are no such restraints concerning the tower and the steps.

So sharp are the ears of Gugs, that our bare feet might readily be heard...

...and it would take but little time for the striding giants to overtake us on those cyclopean steps.

The great stone door was reached at last. To open so vast a thing completely was not to be thought of, but the ghouls hoped to get it up just enough to slip the gravestone under as a prop.

Mighty was the straining of those three ghouls at the stone of the door, and I helped push with as much strength as I had.

Suddenly our desperation was magnified a thousand fold by a sound on the steps below.

Knowing the ways of Gugs, the ghouls set to with something of a frenzy.

GWRRRRRRRRLLLLL

RRAAARGHHH!!

HELP ME!

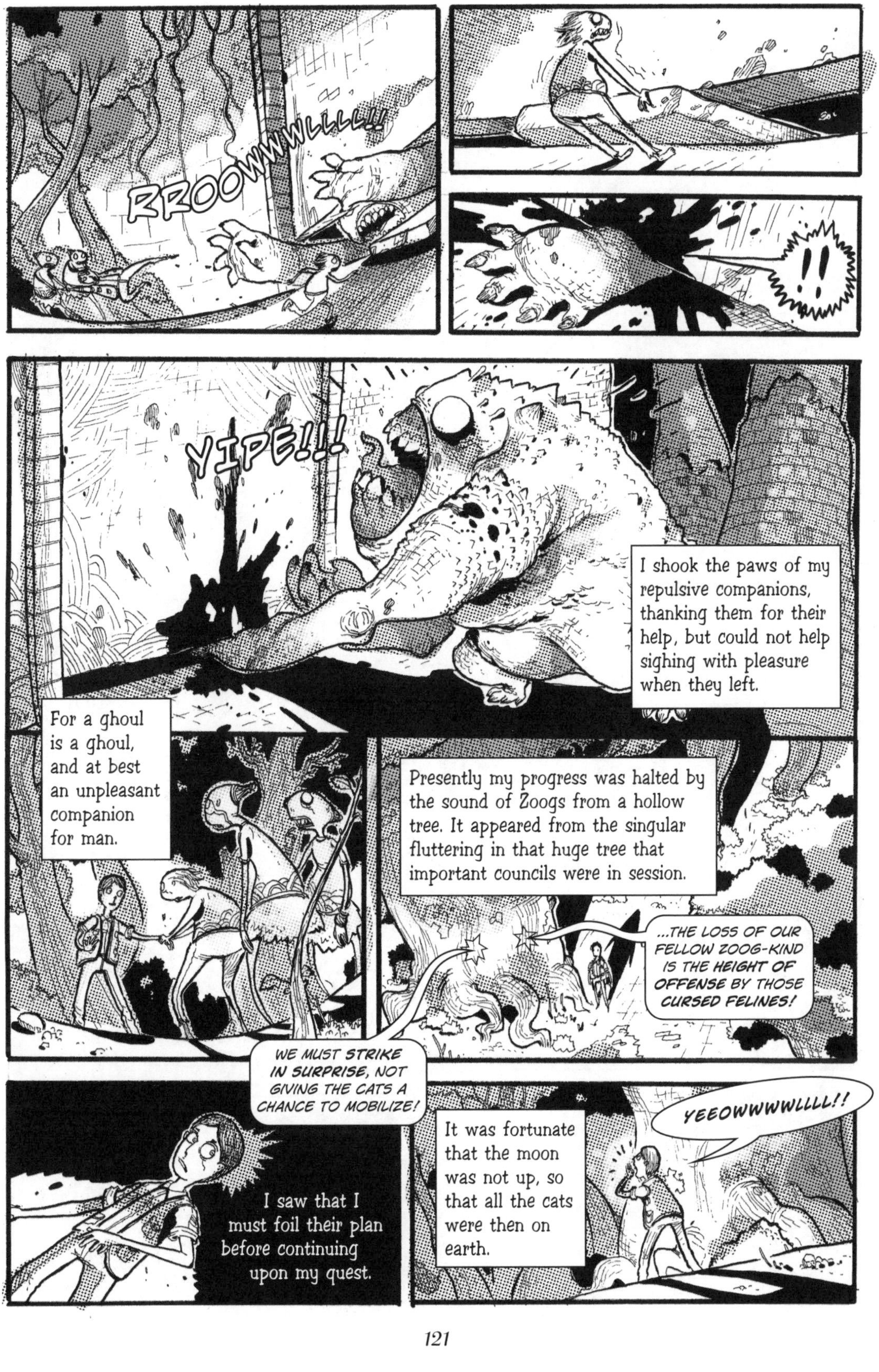
RROOWWWLLLL!!
!!
YIPE!!!
I shook the paws of my repulsive companions, thanking them for their help, but could not help sighing with pleasure when they left.
For a ghoul is a ghoul, and at best an unpleasant companion for man.
Presently my progress was halted by the sound of Zoogs from a hollow tree. It appeared from the singular fluttering in that huge tree that important councils were in session.
...THE LOSS OF OUR FELLOW ZOOG-KIND IS THE HEIGHT OF OFFENSE BY THOSE CURSED FELINES!
WE MUST STRIKE IN SURPRISE, NOT GIVING THE CATS A CHANCE TO MOBILIZE!
I saw that I must foil their plan before continuing upon my quest.
It was fortunate that the moon was not up, so that all the cats were then on earth.
YEEOWWWWLLLL!!

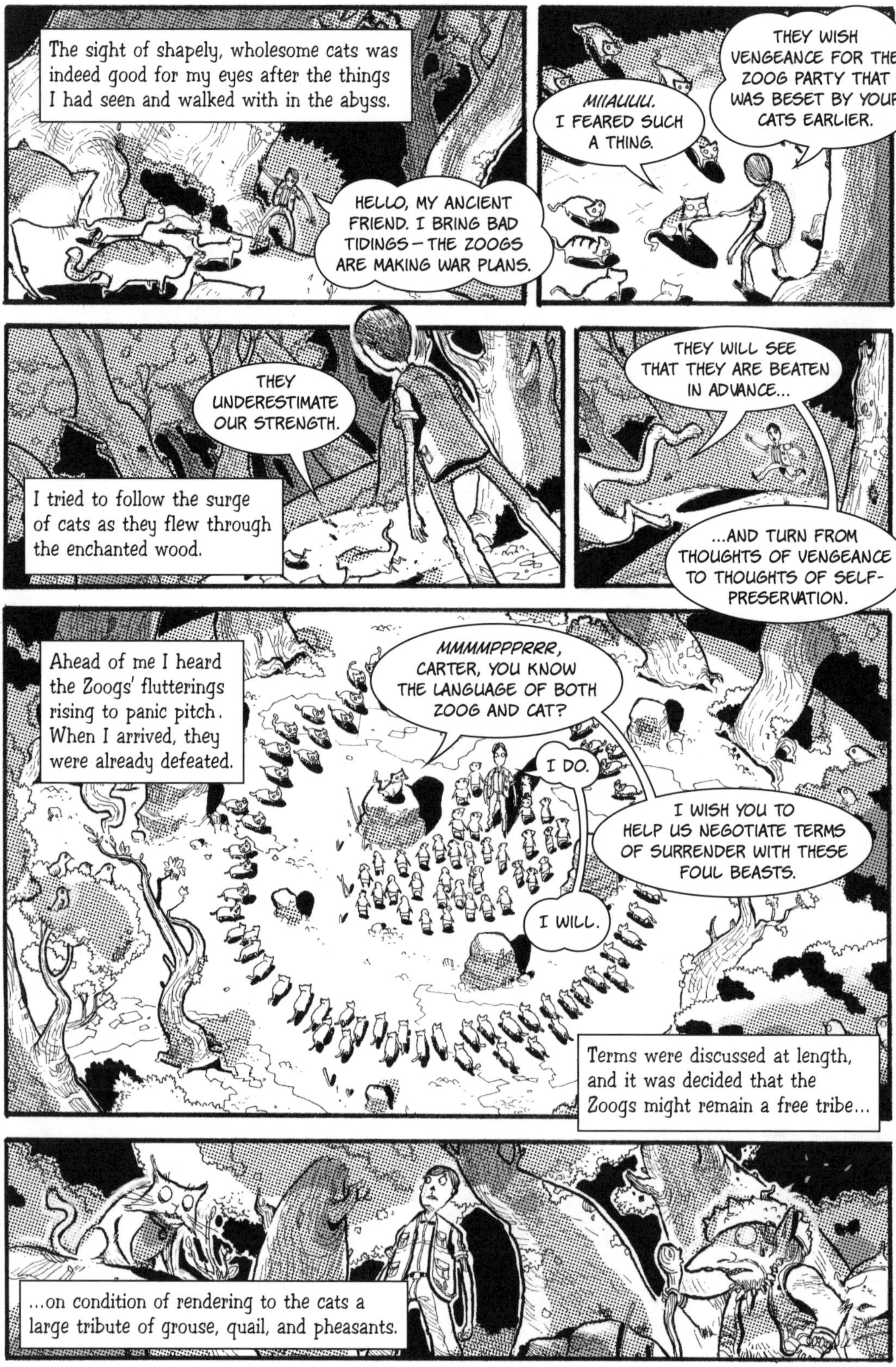

The sight of shapely, wholesome cats was indeed good for my eyes after the things I had seen and walked with in the abyss.
HELLO, MY ANCIENT FRIEND. I BRING BAD TIDINGS—THE ZOOGS ARE MAKING WAR PLANS.
MIIAUUU. I FEARED SUCH A THING.
THEY WISH VENGEANCE FOR THE ZOOG PARTY THAT WAS BESET BY YOUR CATS EARLIER.
THEY UNDERESTIMATE OUR STRENGTH.
I tried to follow the surge of cats as they flew through the enchanted wood.
THEY WILL SEE THAT THEY ARE BEATEN IN ADVANCE...
...AND TURN FROM THOUGHTS OF VENGEANCE TO THOUGHTS OF SELF-PRESERVATION.
Ahead of me I heard the Zoogs' flutterings rising to panic pitch. When I arrived, they were already defeated.
MMMMPPPRRR, CARTER, YOU KNOW THE LANGUAGE OF BOTH ZOOG AND CAT?
I DO.
I WISH YOU TO HELP US NEGOTIATE TERMS OF SURRENDER WITH THESE FOUL BEASTS.
I WILL.
Terms were discussed at length, and it was decided that the Zoogs might remain a free tribe...
...on condition of rendering to the cats a large tribute of grouse, quail, and pheasants.

FRIEND CARTER, I WISH TO OFFER YOU WHATEVER HELP I MAY IN YOUR QUEST.

GIVE MY PASSWORD TO THE OLD CHIEF CAT IN CELEPHAIS, WHERE YOU ARE BOUND.

WHAT CAN YOU TELL ME OF THE STRANGE MEN WITH LONG, NARROW EYES, LONG-LOBED EARS, THIN NOSES, AND POINTED CHINS?

THEM THAT COME IN SWIFT SHIPS FROM THE NORTH AND TRADE *ONYX?*

I bade my friends a reluctant farewell, and I boarded a galleon bound for Celephais.

NAUGHT BUT THAT THEY SELDOM TALK AND COME FROM *INQUANOK.*

NOT MANY PEOPLE CARE TO GO THITHER BECAUSE IT IS A COLD *TWILIGHT* LAND!

At Celephais I did not at once enter the city, but stayed by the seaward wall among traders and sailors.

I then sought the old chief of Celephais' cats.

The furry patriarch was very cordial and communicative.

MIAAAUUUU... *INQUANOK* HOLDS SHADOWS WHICH NO CAT CAN ENDURE AND IN THAT FAR LAND THERE BROODS A HINT OF *OUTER SPACE* WHICH CATS DO NOT LIKE, AND TO WHICH WE ARE MORE SENSITIVE THAN MEN.

THE *GREAT ONES* ARE VERY DANGEROUS CREATURES TO SEEK OUT, AND THE *OTHER GODS* HAVE STRANGE WAYS OF PROTECTING THEM FROM IMPERTINENT CURIOSITY.

BEWARE THE CRAWLING CHAOS *NYARLATHOTEP,* AND NEVER APPROACH THE CENTRAL VOID WHERE THE DAEMON SULTAN *AZATHOTH* GNAWS HUNGRILY IN THE DARK.

ALTOGETHER, IF THE GODS PERSISTENTLY DENY ALL ACCESS TO THE MARVELOUS *SUNSET CITY,* IT IS BETTER *NOT* TO SEEK THAT CITY.

Nevertheless, when the longed-for ship put in, and strange-faced sailors and traders began to appear in the taverns, I gained passage on their vessel.

I AM AN OLD ONYX MINER, WISHFUL TO WORK IN YOUR QUARRIES.

I did not know how much dim supernal memory might fill those children of the Great Ones, and I was sure it would not be wise to tell them of my quest.

The sailors talked of the quarries in which I said I was going to work.

WHAT OF THE *NORTH?* I HEAR OF A COLD DESERT...

HRMM. I'VE HEARD TELL OF AN ANCIENT QUARRY FROM WHICH HAD BEEN HEWN SUCH PRODIGIOUS BLOCKS THAT THE SIGHT OF THEIR CHISELED VACANCIES STRUCK *TERROR* TO ALL WHO BEHELD.

I was moved to deep thought, for I knew from old tales that the Great Ones' castle atop unknown Kadath is of onyx.

Each day the sun wheeled lower and lower in the sky, and the mists overhead grew thicker and thicker. And in two weeks there was not any sunlight at all.

Finally, the ship anchored beside a jutting quay of stone.

The captain of the ship brought me to an old sea tavern where flocked the mariners of many countries.

Far in the shadows of that tavern I saw a squat form I did not like...

...for it was unmistakably that of the old merchant I had seen in the taverns of Dylath-Leen!

124

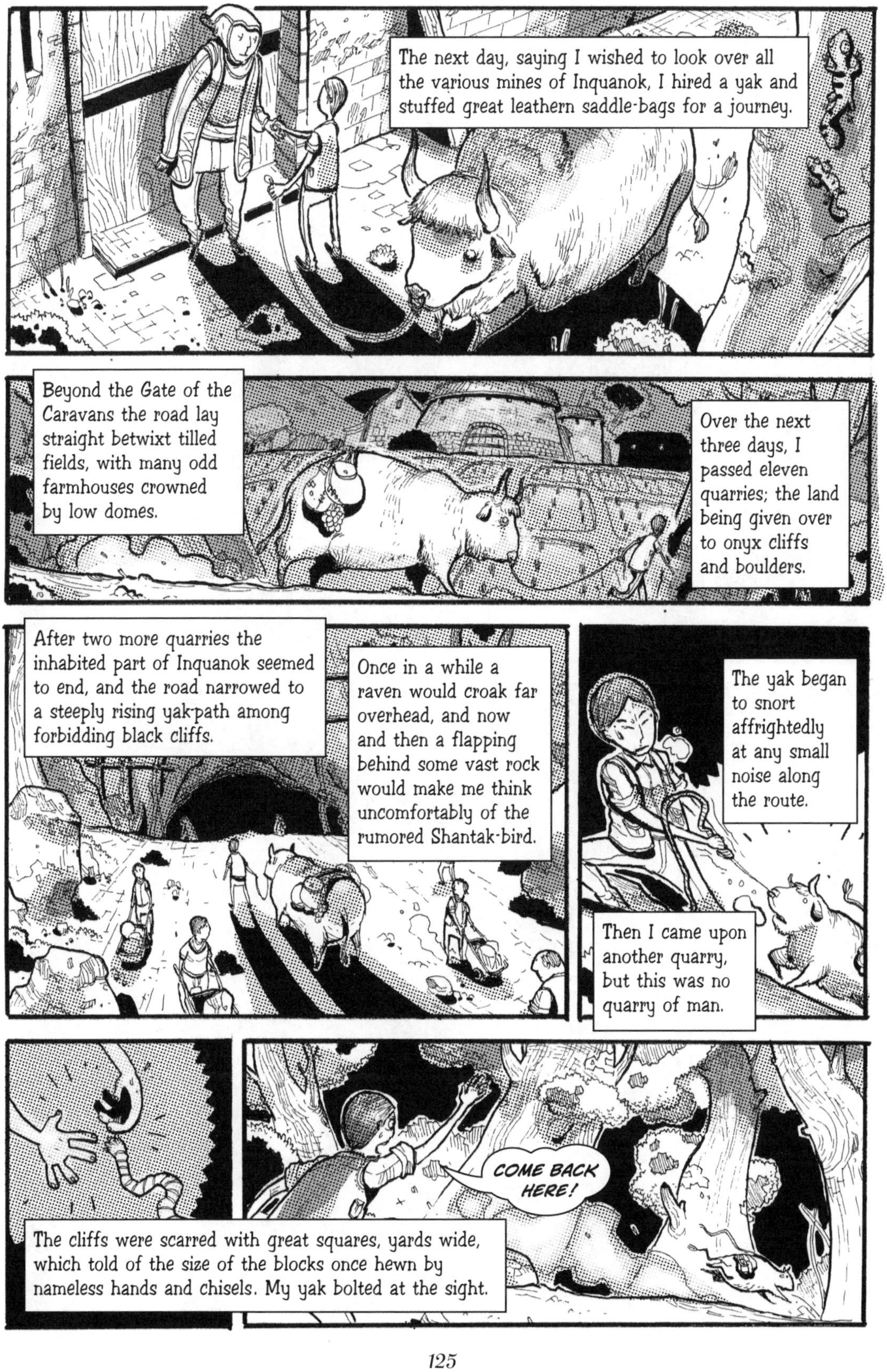
The next day, saying I wished to look over all the various mines of Inquanok, I hired a yak and stuffed great leathern saddle-bags for a journey.
Beyond the Gate of the Caravans the road lay straight betwixt tilled fields, with many odd farmhouses crowned by low domes.
Over the next three days, I passed eleven quarries; the land being given over to onyx cliffs and boulders.
After two more quarries the inhabited part of Inquanok seemed to end, and the road narrowed to a steeply rising yak-path among forbidding black cliffs.
Once in a while a raven would croak far overhead, and now and then a flapping behind some vast rock would make me think uncomfortably of the rumored Shantak-bird.
The yak began to snort affrightedly at any small noise along the route.
Then I came upon another quarry, but this was no quarry of man.
The cliffs were scarred with great squares, yards wide, which told of the size of the blocks once hewn by nameless hands and chisels. My yak bolted at the sight.
COME BACK HERE!

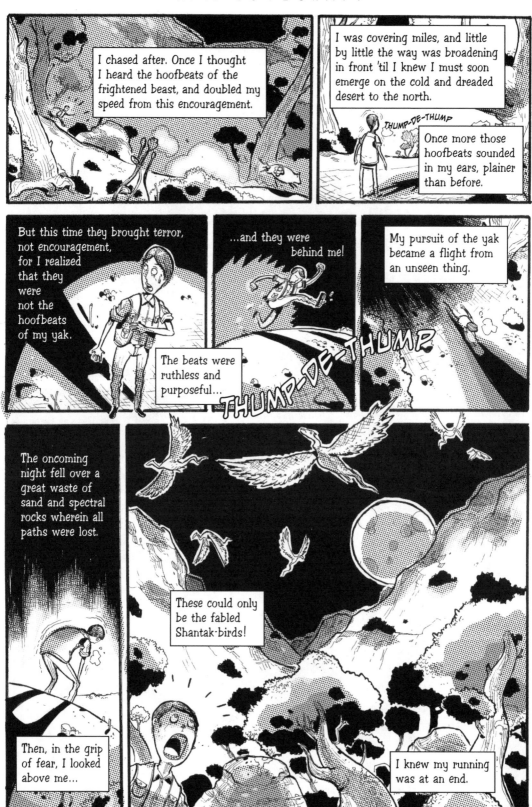

I chased after. Once I thought I heard the hoofbeats of the frightened beast, and doubled my speed from this encouragement.

I was covering miles, and little by little the way was broadening in front 'til I knew I must soon emerge on the cold and dreaded desert to the north.

THUMP-DE-THUMP

Once more those hoofbeats sounded in my ears, plainer than before.

But this time they brought terror, not encouragement, for I realized that they were not the hoofbeats of my yak.

The beats were ruthless and purposeful...

...and they were behind me!

My pursuit of the yak became a flight from an unseen thing.

THUMP-DE-THUMP

The oncoming night fell over a great waste of sand and spectral rocks wherein all paths were lost.

These could only be the fabled Shantak-birds!

Then, in the grip of fear, I looked above me...

I knew my running was at an end.

WE MEET AGAIN, MR. CARTER...

PLEASE — CLIMB ABOARD.

There followed a hideous whirl through frigid space.

And I knew our heading: that haunted place of evil and mystery which is Leng.

Below, I saw gathered the same dark folk who had shanghaied me to the moon on their noisome galley.

And then, I found myself in that most dreadful of all places—

The prehistoric monastery wherein dwells the High-Priest Not To Be Described, which wears a yellow silken mask over its face and prays to the Other Gods and their crawling chaos Nyarlathotep.

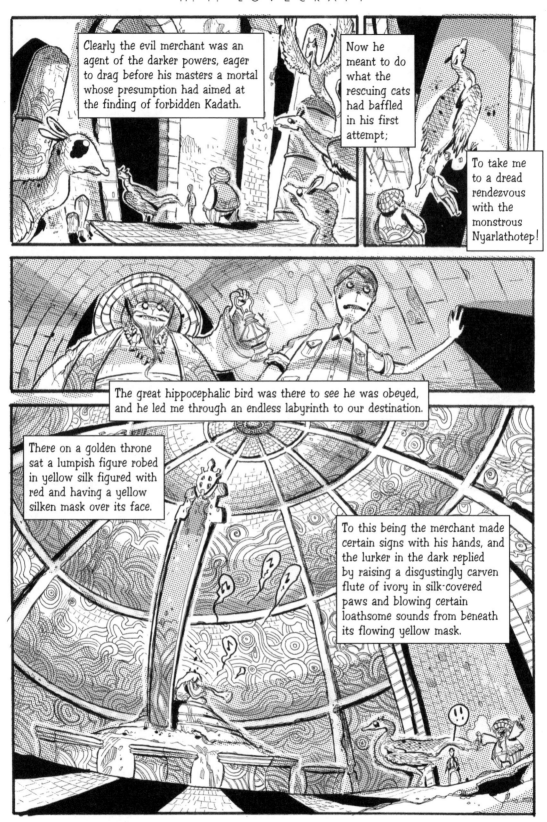

Clearly the evil merchant was an agent of the darker powers, eager to drag before his masters a mortal whose presumption had aimed at the finding of forbidden Kadath.

Now he meant to do what the rescuing cats had baffled in his first attempt;

To take me to a dread rendezvous with the monstrous Nyarlathotep!

The great hippocephalic bird was there to see he was obeyed, and he led me through an endless labyrinth to our destination.

There on a golden throne sat a lumpish figure robed in yellow silk figured with red and having a yellow silken mask over its face.

To this being the merchant made certain signs with his hands, and the lurker in the dark replied by raising a disgustingly carven flute of ivory in silk-covered paws and blowing certain loathsome sounds from beneath its flowing yellow mask.

Then the figured silk slipped a trifle from one of the grayish-white paws —

— and in that hideous second, stark fear drove me to something my reason would never have dared to attempt.

There was in my mind only the instant need to get away from that wriggling, silk-robed monstrosity.

AIEEEEEEEEEEEEEEEEEEEE!!!

I darted out into the labyrinths...

...racing this way and that as chance determined...

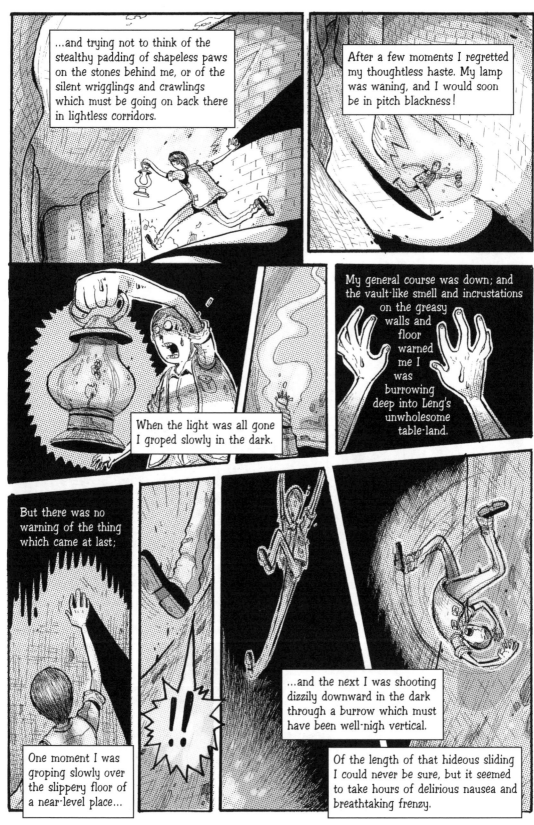

...and trying not to think of the stealthy padding of shapeless paws on the stones behind me, or of the silent wrigglings and crawlings which must be going on back there in lightless corridors.

After a few moments I regretted my thoughtless haste. My lamp was waning, and I would soon be in pitch blackness!

When the light was all gone I groped slowly in the dark.

My general course was down; and the vault-like smell and incrustations on the greasy walls and floor warned me I was burrowing deep into Leng's unwholesome table-land.

But there was no warning of the thing which came at last;

One moment I was groping slowly over the slippery floor of a near-level place...

...and the next I was shooting dizzily downward in the dark through a burrow which must have been well-nigh vertical.

Of the length of that hideous sliding I could never be sure, but it seemed to take hours of delirious nausea and breathtaking frenzy.

130

I could not return from whence I came unaided. I was able to ascertain that the ruined city I found myself in was Sarkomand, which lay near the land of the ghouls.

To continue my journey would require passage over the sea...

Then I finally halted, with the phosphorescent clouds of a northern night shining sickly above me.

But I espied something I could not have hoped for...

The crew huddled about a fire. Some of the almost-human slaves heated iron spears in the flames, at intervals applying their white-hot points to three tightly trussed, writhing prisoners.

...then found that I need not have hoped. I paused in terror when I saw that the ship was one of the dreaded black galleys from the moon.

I recognized the frantic meeping. The tortured ghouls were the faithful trio which had guided me safely from the abyss.

NNNN...

Those ghouls had helped me — saved my life —

And this being Sarkomand, I recalled how near I was to the gates of the ghouls' kingdom.

At length, I found a small company and glibbered my message...

Four of them departed at once, to spread the news to others and gather such troops as might be needed.

NIGHT-GAUNTS? WHAT BUSINESS HAVE THOSE VILE CREATURES HERE?

In time there appeared that proud and influential ghoul which was once the artist Richard Pickman.

THEY. ARE. OUR. STEEDS.

COME!

Then I found myself taken up by the damp, slippery paws.

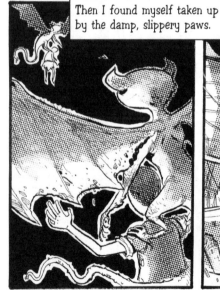

As we approached the noisome camp, a horde of the mephitic moonbeasts began to pour from the evil galleon.

THERE! DOWN THERE!

NIGHT-GAUNTS! NOW!

LET FLY YOUR JAVELINS!

The hellish flutes of the invaders had now begun to whine.

The swelling meeps of the ghouls and the bestial howls of the almost-humans gradually joined the hellish whine of the flutes to form a frantic and indescribable chaos of daemon cacophony.

The fury of the battle increased, and more and more beings fell into nameless extinction.

133

PICKMAN, I DESIRE TO FLY TO THE *ONYX CASTLE*, AND AM SURE THAT THE NIGHT-GAUNTS COULD TAKE ME THITHER. A FLOCK OF TEN TO FIFTEEN —

YOU. HAVE. HELPED. US. WE. SHALL. HELP. YOU.

NOT. TEN. THOUGH. NOT. FIF. TEEN.

ALL.

And there we found, capping the most measureless of mountains, a castle beyond all mortal thought.

We crossed the onyx mines of Inquanok— this time continuing on rather than detouring to that profane monastery of the High-Priest Not to Be Described.

Then I knew that my quest was done, and that I saw above me the goal of all forbidden steps and audacious visions; the fabulous home of the Great Ones atop unknown Kadath.

I had come to unknown Kadath in the cold waste, but I had not found the gods. Earth's gods were not there.

As I reflected upon these things, there rang without warning through that pale-litten and limitless chamber the hideous blast of a daemon trumpet.

Three times pealed that frightful brazen scream, and when the echoes of the third blast had died away —

I was alone.

Presently from the chamber's uttermost reaches a new sound came. In this low fanfare echoed all the wonder and melody of ethereal dream, and odors of incense came to match the golden notes.

Then down the wide lane betwixt the two columns a lone figure strode.

He spoke, and in his melodious tones there rippled the wild music of Lethean streams.

RANDOLPH CARTER, YOU HAVE COME TO SEE THE GREAT ONES WHOM IT IS UNLAWFUL FOR MEN TO SEE.

BUT YOU, RANDOLPH CARTER, HAVE BRAVED ALL THINGS OF EARTH'S DREAM-LAND, AND BURN STILL WITH THE FLAME OF QUEST.

YOU CAME NOT AS ONE CURIOUS, BUT AS ONE SEEKING HIS DUE, NOR HAVE YOU FAILED EVER IN REVERENCE TOWARD THE MILD GODS OF EARTH.

BUT THEY ARE GONE FROM THEIR CASTLE ON UNKNOWN KADATH...

TO DWELL IN YOUR MARVELOUS CITY!

YOU HAVE DREAMED TOO WELL, O ARCH-DREAMER, FOR YOU HAVE DRAWN DREAM'S GODS AWAY FROM THE WORLD OF ALL MEN'S VISIONS TO THAT WHICH IS WHOLLY YOURS; HAVING BUILDED OUT OF YOUR BOYHOOD'S SMALL FANCIES A CITY MORE LOVELY THAN ALL THE PHANTOMS THAT HAVE GONE BEFORE!

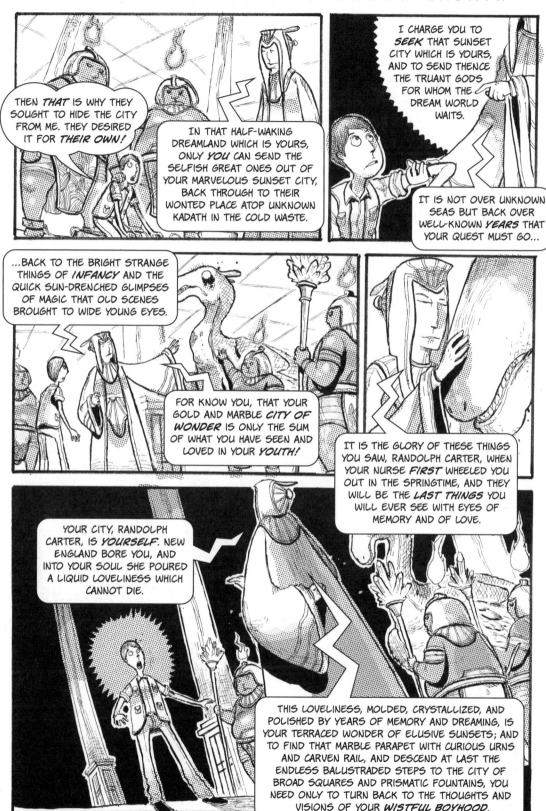

THEN *THAT* IS WHY THEY SOUGHT TO HIDE THE CITY FROM ME. THEY DESIRED IT FOR *THEIR OWN!*

IN THAT HALF-WAKING DREAMLAND WHICH IS YOURS, ONLY *YOU* CAN SEND THE SELFISH GREAT ONES OUT OF YOUR MARVELOUS SUNSET CITY, BACK THROUGH TO THEIR WONTED PLACE ATOP UNKNOWN KADATH IN THE COLD WASTE.

I CHARGE YOU TO *SEEK* THAT SUNSET CITY WHICH IS YOURS, AND TO SEND THENCE THE TRUANT GODS FOR WHOM THE DREAM WORLD WAITS.

IT IS NOT OVER UNKNOWN SEAS BUT BACK OVER WELL-KNOWN *YEARS* THAT YOUR QUEST MUST GO...

...BACK TO THE BRIGHT STRANGE THINGS OF *INFANCY* AND THE QUICK SUN-DRENCHED GLIMPSES OF MAGIC THAT OLD SCENES BROUGHT TO WIDE YOUNG EYES.

FOR KNOW YOU, THAT YOUR GOLD AND MARBLE *CITY OF WONDER* IS ONLY THE SUM OF WHAT YOU HAVE SEEN AND LOVED IN YOUR *YOUTH!*

IT IS THE GLORY OF THESE THINGS YOU SAW, RANDOLPH CARTER, WHEN YOUR NURSE *FIRST* WHEELED YOU OUT IN THE SPRINGTIME, AND THEY WILL BE THE *LAST THINGS* YOU WILL EVER SEE WITH EYES OF MEMORY AND OF LOVE.

YOUR CITY, RANDOLPH CARTER, IS *YOURSELF*. NEW ENGLAND BORE YOU, AND INTO YOUR SOUL SHE POURED A LIQUID LOVELINESS WHICH CANNOT DIE.

THIS LOVELINESS, MOLDED, CRYSTALLIZED, AND POLISHED BY YEARS OF MEMORY AND DREAMING, IS YOUR TERRACED WONDER OF ELUSIVE SUNSETS; AND TO FIND THAT MARBLE PARAPET WITH CURIOUS URNS AND CARVEN RAIL, AND DESCEND AT LAST THE ENDLESS BALUSTRADED STEPS TO THE CITY OF BROAD SQUARES AND PRISMATIC FOUNTAINS, YOU NEED ONLY TO TURN BACK TO THE THOUGHTS AND VISIONS OF YOUR *WISTFUL BOYHOOD*.

SEEK OUT YOUR MARVELOUS CITY AND DRIVE THENCE THE RECREANT *GREAT ONES*. SEND THEM BACK GENTLY TO THOSE SCENES WHICH ARE OF THEIR *OWN* YOUTH.

EASIER EVEN THAN THE WAY OF DIM MEMORY IS THE WAY I WILL PREPARE FOR YOU.

STEER FOR THAT BRIGHTEST STAR JUST SOUTH OF THE ZENITH, BUT ONLY 'TIL YOU HEAR A FAR-OFF SINGING IN THE HIGH AETHER. THEN REIN YOUR SHANTAK, FOR HIGHER THAN THAT LURKS *MADNESS*.

THEN YOU WILL SEE YOUR CITY... AND THE *GREAT ONES*.

OVER AND OVER MUST YOU SPEAK TO THE WANDERING GREAT ONES OF THEIR HOME AND YOUTH, 'TIL AT LAST THEY WILL WEEP AND ASK TO BE SHOWN THE RETURNING PATH THEY HAVE FORGOTTEN...

THEN WILL THE MARVELOUS *SUNSET CITY* BE *YOURS* TO CHERISH AND INHABIT *FOREVER*, AND ONCE MORE WILL EARTH'S GODS RULE THE DREAMS OF MEN FROM THEIR ACCUSTOMED SEAT.

HEI! AA-SHANTA 'NYGH! YOU ARE OFF! SEND BACK EARTH'S GODS TO THEIR HAUNTS ON UNKNOWN KADATH, AND PRAY TO ALL SPACE THAT YOU MAY NEVER MEET ME IN MY THOUSAND OTHER FORMS.

FAREWELL, RANDOLPH CARTER, AND *BEWARE*; FOR I AM *NYARLATHOTEP, THE CRAWLING CHAOS!*

Gasping and dizzy on my hideous Shantak, I shot screamingly into space.

Then there fell a hush of portent, and there rose a hint of far-off melody, droning in faint chords that our own universe of stars knows not.

The stars danced mockingly, almost shifting now and then to form pale signs of doom; and ever the winds howled of a blackness and loneliness beyond the cosmos.

And as that music grew, the Shantak raised its ears and plunged ahead, and I likewise bent to catch each lovely strain.

It was a song, but not the song of any voice. Night and the spheres sang it, and it was old when space and Nyarlathotep and the Other Gods were born.

Then came, too late, the warning of the evil one, who had told me to beware the madness of that song.

Only to taunt had Nyarlathotep marked out the way to safety and the marvelous sunset city; only to mock had that black messenger revealed the secret of the truant gods, whose steps he could easily lead back at will!

For madness and the void's wild vengeance are Nyarlathotep's only gifts to the presumptuous.

Unswerving and obedient to the foul legate's orders, that hellish bird plunged onward, darting meteor-like toward chambers beyond time wherein Azathoth gnaws shapeless and ravenous.

But too well had Nyarlathotep planned his mocking and his tantalizing, for he had reminded me of that which no gusts of icy terror could quite efface —

Home —
New England —
Beacon Hill —
the waking world.

"For know you, that your gold and marble city of wonder is only the sum of what you have seen and loved in youth..."

"To find that marble parapet... and descend at last those endless balustraded steps to the city... you need only to turn back to the thoughts and visions of your wistful boyhood..."

Onward— onward— dizzily onward to ultimate doom through the blackness where sightless feelers pawed and slimy snouts jostled and nameless things tittered.

But the image and the thought had come, and I knew clearly that I was only dreaming, and that somewhere the world of waking and the city of my infancy still lay.

Words came again —
"You need only turn back to the thoughts and visions of your wistful boyhood."

Thick though the rushing nightmare that clutched my senses, I could turn, and if I chose I could leap off the evil Shantak...

I could leap off and dare those depths of night that yawned interminably down, those depths of fear whose terrors yet could not exceed the nameless doom that lurked waiting at chaos' core.

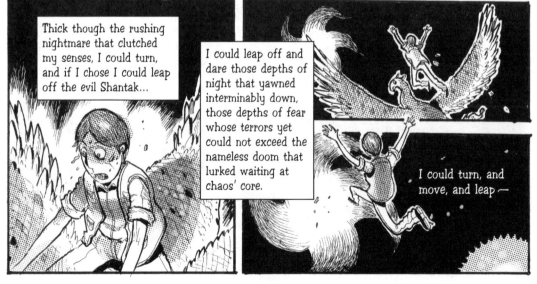

I could turn, and move, and leap —

Aeons reeled, universes died and were born again, stars became nebulae and nebulae became stars, and still I fell through those endless voids of sentient blackness.

Matter and light were born anew as space once had known them; and comets, suns and worlds sprang flaming into life, always and always, back to the beginning.

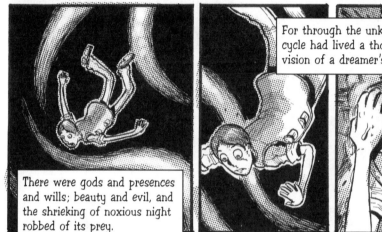

There were gods and presences and wills; beauty and evil, and the shrieking of noxious night robbed of its prey.

For through the unknown ultimate cycle had lived a thought and a vision of a dreamer's boyhood.

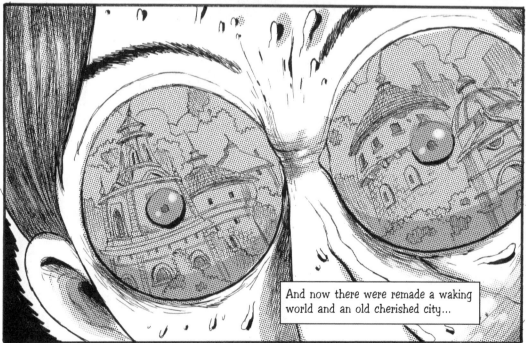

And now there were remade a waking world and an old cherished city...

I had indeed descended at last the wide marmoreal flights to my marvelous city, for I was come again to the fair New England world that had wrought me.

The machinations of the crawling chaos Nyarlathotep were behind me.

No doubt, he taunted insolently the mild gods of earth, snatching them abruptly and of his own power from their scented revels in the marvelous sunset city.

But I had thwarted his plans and succeeded in my own, finally finding the marvelous city...

HOME.

SKOT OLSEN (front cover, page 11)

While growing up in Connecticut, Skot and his parents spent their summers sailing up and down the coast of New England and all over the West Indies. It was on these long trips that he developed his love for the sea which forms the basis for much of his work. A graduate of the Joe Kubert School of Cartoon and Graphic Art, Skot now lives on the edge of the Florida Everglades, where he concentrates on paintings which have been featured in numerous publications and exhibited in galleries in Florida, New York and California. His illustrations are printed in *Graphic Classics: Edgar Allan Poe*, *Graphic Classics: H.P. Lovecraft*, *Graphic Classics: Bram Stoker* and *Adventure Classics*, and a large collection of his work is online at www.skotolsen.com.

LEONG WAN KOK (back cover, pages 1, 96)

Leong Wan Kok, known to Malaysian comic readers as Puyuh, was born in Malaysia in the year of the rabbit. He now lives in Kuala Lumpur. Leong has been active in the comics industry in Malaysia since 2002, when he was invited to represent his country in the "Asia in Comics" festival in Tokyo. *The Oval Portrait*, in *Graphic Classics: Edgar Allan Poe*, was his first work published in the U.S. In December 2006, his book of illustrations and comics, *Astro Cityzen*, was released in Malaysia. "This is a project that has taken seven months of my time and is my labor of love," says Kok. You can see more of his work online at www.1000tentacles.com.

LORD DUNSANY (page 2)

Lord Dunsany, born Edward John Moreton Drax Plunkett, wrote more than 70 books, beginning with *The Gods of Pergana* in 1905. He was one of the most popular fantasy authors in the English language and also a poet, a successful playwright, and a competitive chess player. *After the Fire* first appeared in his 1915 collection *Fifty-One Tales*. Dunsany died in Dublin in 1957. H.P. Lovecraft was a great admirer of his stories, and wrote of Dunsany: "To the truly imaginative he is a talisman and a key unlocking rich storehouses of dream."

RACHEL MASILAMANI (page 2)

Rachel Masilamani lives in Pittsburgh, PA. Her stories have appeared in comics anthologies, literary magazines, textbooks, and in her self-published series, *RPM Comics*. The first issue of *RPM Comics* in 2000 received a grant from the Xeric Foundation, a nonprofit corporation founded by Teenage Mutant Turtles creator Peter Laird. The Foundation offers financial assistance to self-publishing comics creators. She is also a graduate student in library science at the University of Pittsburgh, where she writes and researches about the connections between visual literacy and information literacy. Rachel's adaptation of *After Twenty Years* is in *Graphic Classics: O. Henry*. You can contact her at rpm77@lycos.com.

LANCE TOOKS (pages 3, 58)

As an animator for fifteen years, as well as a comics artist, Lance Tooks' work has appeared in more than a hundred television commercials, films and music videos. He has self-published the comics *Divided by Infinity Danger Funnies* and *Muthafucka*. His stories have appeared in *Zuzu*, *Shade*, *Vibe*, *Girltalk*, *World War 3 Illustrated*, *Floaters*, *Pure Friction*, the Italian magazine *Lupo Alberto*, *Graphic Classics: Ambrose Bierce*, *Graphic Classics: Edgar Allan Poe*, *Graphic Classics: Mark Twain* and *Graphic Classics: Robert Louis Stevenson*. He also illustrated *The Black Panthers for* *Beginners*, written by Herb Boyd. Lance's first graphic novel, *Narcissa*, was named one of the best books of 2002 by *Publisher's Weekly*, and he has recently completed his *Lucifer's Garden of Verses* series for NBM ComicsLit. In 2004 Lance moved from his native New York to Madrid, Spain, where he married and has recently finished a Spanish translation of *Narcissa*.

ROD LOTT (pages 4, 11)

Oklahoma City resident Rod Lott is a freelance writer and graphic designer involved in advertising and journalism. For twelve years, he has published and edited the more-or-less quarterly magazine *Hitch: The Journal of Pop Culture Absurdity* (www.hitchmagazine.com), and edits *Bookgasm*, a daily book review and news site at www.bookgasm.com. Rod's humorous essays have been published in several anthologies, including *May Contain Nuts* and *101 Damnations*. He has scripted comics adaptations of stories by Edgar Allan Poe, Clark Ashton Smith, Sax Rohmer, H.G. Wells, H.P. Lovecraft, O. Henry, Rafael Sabatini and Le Fanu for *Graphic Classics*, and is now scripting a comics adaptation of Bierce's *The Damned Thing* for the new edition of *Graphic Classics: Ambrose Bierce*. You can learn more about Rod's work online at www.rodlott.com.

MARK A. NELSON (page 4)

Mark Nelson was a professor of art at Northern Illinois University for twenty years. From 1998 to 2004 he was a senior artist at Raven Software, doing conceptual work, painting digital skins and creating textures for computer games. Mark is now the lead instructor of the Animation Department of Madison Area Technical College in Madison, Wisconsin. His comics credits include *Blood and Shadows* for DC, *Aliens* for Dark Horse Comics, and *Feud* for Marvel. He has worked for numerous publishers, and his art is represented in *Spectrum #4, 5, 6, 8, 10* and his art collections *From Pencils to Inks: The Art of Mark A. Nelson* (2004) and *Strange Thoughts and Random Images* (2008). Mark's comics and illustrations have appeared in *Graphic Classics: Edgar Allan Poe*, *Graphic Classics: Arthur Conan Doyle*, *Graphic Classics: H.P. Lovecraft*, *Graphic Classics: Ambrose Bierce*, *Graphic Classics: Jack London*, *Graphic Classics: O. Henry*, *Graphic Classics: Bram Stoker*, *Horror Classics*, *Rosebud 18* and *The Best of Rosebud*, all from Eureka Productions.

MARY SHELLEY (page 11)

Mary Wollstonecraft Godwin was the daughter of anarchist political writer William Godwin and feminist author Mary Wollstonecraft. She met poet Percy Bysshe Shelley when she was sixteen, and Shelley became a follower of her father's atheist philosophy. Mary eloped with the then-married Shelley in 1814, and bore him two children prior to the events retold here in *Fantasmagoriana*. In December 1816, shortly following the suicide of Shelley's first wife, the couple married and in 1818 *Frankenstein; or, The Modern Prometheus* first saw print. She authored a number of other novels, as well as short stories, biographies and travel books, but none approached the popular success of *Frankenstein*.

NATHANIEL HAWTHORNE (page 58)

Born in 1804 in Salem, Massachusetts, Nathaniel Hawthorne was the great-grandson of a prosecutor in the Salem Witch Trials, which provided the inspiration for a number of of his stories, including *The House of Seven Gables*. He was a friend of many prominent New Englanders including Henry Wadsworth Longfellow,

Ralph Waldo Emerson, Henry David Thoreau and Amos Bronson Alcott, father of Louisa May Alcott. In 1841 he became a part of the Transcendentalist movement, which influenced his later writings, including his most famous novel, *The Scarlet Letter*. *Rappaccini's Daughter* was written in 1844 and published in Hawthorne's short story collection *Mosses from an Old Manse*.

L. FRANK BAUM (page 80)

After a series of failed businesses, Lyman Frank Baum's first success as an author came at age 41 with *Mother Goose in Prose*, published in 1897. He followed that with *Father Goose: His Book*, and in 1900 published *The Wonderful Wizard of Oz* to great acclaim. Baum wrote a large number of other fantasy books, travel books and novels for adults, and a series of books for girls under the pen name "Edith Van Dyne." None equaled the popularity of his Oz books, and in 1911 Baum declared bankruptcy. He then decided to concentrate on the Oz series, and produced one Oz book per year until his death in 1919.

ANTONELLA CAPUTO (page 80)

Antonella was born and raised in Rome, Italy, and now lives in Lancaster, England. She has been an architect, archaeologist, art restorer, photographer, calligrapher, interior designer, theater designer, actress and theater director. Her first published work was *Casa Montesi*, a fortnightly comic strip which appeared in the national magazine *Il Giornalino*. She has since written comedies for children and scripts for comics and magazines in the UK, Europe and the U.S. She works with Nick Miller as the writing half of Team Sputnik, and has collaborated with Nick and other artists in the *Graphic Classics* volumes *Edgar Allan Poe*, *Arthur Conan Doyle*, *H. G. Wells*, *Jack London*, *Ambrose Bierce*, *Mark Twain*, *O. Henry*, *Rafael Sabatini*, *Horror Classics*, *Adventure Classics* and *Gothic Classics*.

BRAD TEARE (page 80)

Utah artist Brad Teare maintains a career as both an illustrator and a fine arts painter and woodcut artist. Clients include *The New York Times*, *Fortune* and Random House, where he illustrated for authors such as James Michener, Ann Tyler, and Alice Walker. Teare's comics creations have appeared in *Heavy Metal* magazine and the *Big Book* series from Paradox Press. He is the author of the graphic novel *Cypher* from Peregrine Smith Books (excerpted in *Rosebud 20*). Brad's work can be viewed online at www.officialcypherfansite.com and www.bradteare.com.

CLARK ASHTON SMITH (page 95)

A self-educated Californian, Clark Ashton Smith began writing fiction at age eleven, though most of his early writings were poetry. On the publication of his first poems in 1911, he was hailed as "the new Keats" by the San Francisco press, and became friends with Ambrose Bierce, Jack London and George Sterling. Despite the early success, and due to ill health, Smith chose to maintain a quiet, solitary life in rural California. Smith's first horror story was published in *The Overland Monthly* in 1925, and during the 1930s he produced about a hundred fantasy stories for the pulp magazines, especially *Weird Tales*. His work drew the attention of H.P. Lovecraft, with whom Smith corresponded until Lovecraft's death in 1937. After that date, Smith wrote little weird fiction, but concentrated on his poetry and artwork until his death in 1961. He is now considered one of the greatest fantasy poets of the 20th century.

An adaptation of Smith's *The Beasts of Averoigne* appears in *Horror Classics*.

EVERT GERADTS (page 95)

Evert Geradts is a Dutch comics artist now living in Toulouse, France. One of the founders of the Dutch underground comix scene, he started the influential magazine *Tante Leny Presents*, in which appeared his first *Sailears & Susie* stories. He is a disciple of Carl Barks, whom he names "the Aesop of the 20th century." Over the years Geradts has written about a thousand stories featuring Donald Duck and other Disney characters for Dutch comics. He also writes stories for the popular comic series *Sjors & Sjimmie* and *De Muziekbuurters*. Evert's work appears in *Graphic Classics: Ambrose Bierce*, *Graphic Classics: Bram Stoker*, *Graphic Classics: Edgar Allan Poe* and *Graphic Classics: Robert Louis Stevenson*.

H.P. LOVECRAFT (page 96)

Howard Phillips Lovecraft was born in Providence, Rhode Island in 1890. His father died in 1898, and his mother suffered from mental instability until her death in 1921. Poor health and his neurotic, overprotective mother combined to make something of a recluse of Lovecraft. Growing up, he had little contact with other children, and as an adult maintained his many long-distance relationships through voluminous correspondence. He was obsessed with dreams, and wrote most of his stories and poems around a central theme of ancient gods who once ruled the earth and are merely awaiting a return to power. His writings appeared mostly in the "pulp" magazines of his time and received little critical attention outside of the horror genre. Since Lovecraft's death in 1937, his stories have grown in popularity and have spawned a huge cult of both fans and professional writers who continue to expand Lovecraft's themes through stories set in the "Cthulhu Mythos." More stories by Lovecraft appear in *Horror Classics* and *Graphic Classics: H.P. Lovecraft*.

BEN AVERY (page 96)

Ben Avery adapted the script of the critically acclaimed graphic novel *The Hedge Knight* and its sequel *The Sworn Sword*, published by Marvel and based on the novellas by *New York Times* bestselling fantasy author George R.R. Martin. The writer of the *Oz/Wonderland Chronicles*, from BuyMeToys.com and based on the beloved fantasy characters, has worked on Image Comics' *Lullaby* and *The Imaginaries* and his own all-ages series *TimeFlyz* (about time traveling flies). Ben is now scripting a adaptation of Stanley Weinbaum's *A Martian Odyssey* for *Science Fiction Classics*. He lives in Indiana with his wife and four kids, but wishes he lived in a northern Ontario cabin (with his wife and four kids, of course).

TOM POMPLUN

The designer, editor and publisher of *Graphic Classics*, Tom has a background in both fine and commercial art and a lifelong interest in comics. He designed and produced *Rosebud*, a journal of fiction, poetry and illustration, from 1993 to 2003, and in 2001 he founded *Graphic Classics*. Tom is currently working on a revised edition of *Graphic Classics: Ambrose Bierce*, scheduled for August 2008 release, and *Graphic Classics: Oscar Wilde*, for December 2008. The book will feature a new comics adaptation of *The Picture of Dorian Gray*, by British writer Alex Burrows and illustrated by *Graphic Classics* favorite Lisa K. Weber.